# *Storming St. Kilda By Tram*
## *One Man's Attempt To Get Home*

(image: TheatreWorks Archive, Fryer Library)

Written by Paul Davies
Photos by Ruth Maddison
Directed by Mark Shirrefs
Costumes Susan Weiss
Produced by TheatreWorks

A Picture Play

3rd Edition
Published by Gondwana Press, November 2019
Suffolk Park 2481 NSW

First published as a play script in 1991 by Currency Press

This book is copyright. Apart from any fair dealing for the purpose of private study, research or review, as permitted under the Copyright Act, no part may be reproduced by any process without written permission. Inquiries concerning publication, performance translation or recording rights should be addressed to the author.

Any performance or public reading of *Storming St. Kilda By Tram* requires a licence from the author. The purchase of this book in no way gives the purchaser the right to perform the play in public, whether by means of a staged production or a reading.

© The moral right of the author has been asserted.

All performance images © Ruth Madison

National Library of Australia
Cataloguing-in-Publication data
Davies, Paul 1949-
Storming St. Kilda By Train
ISBN 0 86819 269 4

(image: TheatreWorks Archive, Fryer Library)

St. Kilda Mayor Elaine Miller on the running board

# AUTHOR'S NOTE

I am a tram fanatic. I won't beat around the bush. I'm quite addicted to them. When Brisbane stupidly closed its tram system down I moved to Melbourne. Trams don't use petrol, they don't cause pollution and they rarely break down. There is a serenity about tram travel that can't be matched on road transport.

The Melbourne tram on which we've done the show three times now was built before the second world war and is still going strong. If it was a car or a bus it would be in a museum.

This tram has been a silent witness to the full gamut of human behaviour. Within its cosy wooden interior pregnant women have been rushed to hospital, bank robbers have attempted their getaways, fools have fallen in and out of love, laughter has been heard, songs have been sung and scripts like the Tram Show have been written. Our play is an amalgam of all the crazy wonderful things that happen on public transport. In over 300 performances we've never played to less than a packed house and so far we haven't lost a passenger (or cast member thank God!).

When we first ran the Tram Show in 1982 for the Melbourne Moomba Festival, it seemed risky at the time. A mad idea. But strangely enough people liked it. In fact Melbournians flocked to it and those who missed the Tram are constantly begging us to bring it back.

There is no other experience in theatre quite like it. Here we are literally pushing performance into new territory. The action happens all around you and flows with the characters off the tram onto the street, so for many months the "audience" consists not only of the paying customers but thousands of people who witness it as it goes by.

We also find we are attracting overseas tourists and who knows, with a bit of help from you we may soon "Storm the World by Tram".

Since the Tram Show's original production in 1982 Melbourne has seen the flowering of a whole range of plays that take place in real locations; in riverboats, boarding houses, family mansions, magistrates courts, council chambers and botanical gardens.

Now only the Sky is the limit!

Paul Davies

## CONTENTS

| | |
|---|---|
| Introduction | 6 |
| Cast and Characters | 9 |
| Setting and Route | 11 |
| **Storming St. Kilda By Tram**   ACT 1 inward journey | 13 |
| ACT 2 Outward journey | 93 |
| Launch, Malvern Depot | 168 |
| Critical Reception | 170 |
| Author | 204 |
| Dedication | 206 |

# The "*Tram Show*"

What became known as *The Tram Show* was inspired by a real life incident in which a punk, an old drunk, a conductor and two police officers collided to cause mayhem on a late night ride home. It was produced through seven iterations across a dozen years from 1982 to 1994 on various tram routes in both Melbourne and Adelaide.

Over this time *The Tram Show* attracted around twenty thousand passengers to almost 400 performances, generating (on today's figures) roughly a million dollars at the box office. It also trambulated a total distance that would have taken the play and its combined nightly audiences half-way around the world ! An original season timed to coincide with the Moomba Festival in 1982, and expected to run for two weeks, was soon booked out and enjoyed a number of extended seasons to run for over four months – until Melbourne's winter weather (and cast exhaustion) made further performances impractical.

What had started life as *Storming Mont Albert By Tram* in 1982 was revised to become *Storming St.Kilda By Tram* in 1988 and 1991, then *Storming Melbourne By Tram* and *Storming Swanston Walk by Tram* in 1992, and finally *Storming Glenelg By Tram* in 1992 and 1994 – since Adelaide was the only other Australian city with an operating tram system sufficiently large enough to accommodate a ninety minute play in two halves.

During this evolution the cast was cut from nine to seven characters, partly to tighten the story and partly to make it more financially viable on a self-funding basis.

The text was first published by Currency Press in its second iteration as *Storming St. Kilda By Tram* and the same version of the play won an AWGIE (Australian Writer's Guild Award) in 1988. This illustrated edition is the second in a suite of *Tram Show* manuscripts that includes *Storming Mont Albert* and *Storming Glenelg By Tram*. Other picture plays by Paul Davies in the series include the "boat show" *Breaking Up In Balwyn* (1983), the "house shows" *Living Rooms* (1986) and *Full House/No Vacancies* (1989), *Last Train To St. Kilda* (1987) and *On Shifting Sandshoes* (1988)

The *"Tram Show"* is dedicated to the memory of Carolyn Howard who rode with the author on the original tram trip that inspired it all and whose energy, talent, and enthusiasm helped bring TheatreWorks into being and therefore made this play possible.

## Original Production

*Storming St. Kilda By Tram* was originally produced by TheatreWorks as *Storming Mont Albert By Tram* on the Number 42 route in 1982, and developed in collaboration with director, Mark Shirrefs, and the following cast:

| | |
|---|---|
| ALICE | Mary Sitarenos |
| DANNY | Peter Sommerfeld |
| SAMANTHA | Hannie Rayson |
| CATHY | Carolyn Howard |
| NIGEL | Peter Finlay |
| TERRY | Tony Kishawi |
| MORRIS | Paul Davies |
| COPS | Graeme Stephen & Brett Stewart |

In 1988 the play was restaged aboard a Number 69 St.Kilda Tram from 7th March to 22 May as part of the Melbourne Comedy Festival again directed by Mark Shirrefs. It was later taken to Adelaide as *Storming Glenelg By Tram*. Then back to Melbourne as *Storming Swanston Walk By Tram* and *Storming Melbourne's 150$^{th}$ By Tram*.

# CAST

L-R:

Ian Scott (Snr Const. Warren Wilkinson)

Peter Finlay (Nigel Davidson)

Liz Sadler (Alice Katransky)

Caz Howard (Cathy Waterman)

St Kilda Mayor Elaine Miller

Cliff Ellen (Danny O'Rourke)

Jeremy Standford (Terry Meagher)

Rosie Tonkin (Samantha Hart-Byrne)

Howard Stanley ( Morris Stanley)

## CHARACTERS

**ALICE KATRANSKI** (Liz Sadler) a connie, late 20s

**SAMANTHA HART-BYRNE** (Rosie Tonkin) a Brighton housewife, 30s

**DANNY O'ROURKE** (Cliff Ellen) a former political science lecturer 60s

**CATHY WATERMAN** (Carolyn Howard) a mother of two, 35

**NIGEL DAVIDSON** (Peter Finlay) a Sydney "filmmaker" 37

**TERRY MEAGHER** (Jeremy Stanford) a punk, mid-20s

**MORRIS STANLEY** (Howard Stanley) a ticket inspector 40ish

**SNR CONSTABLE WARREN WILKINSON** (Ian Scott) 40ish

**CONSTABLE CYRIL FOSTER** (James Cox) 28 his junior

## SETTING

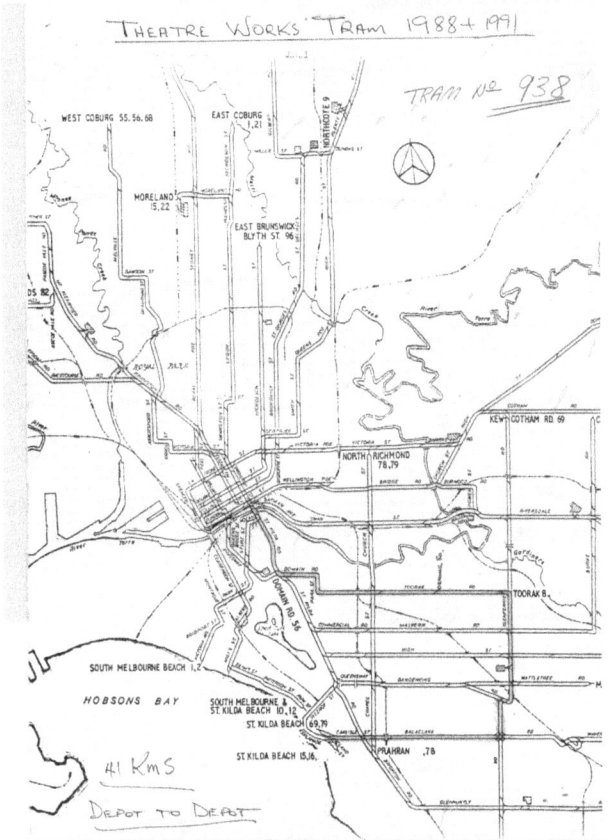

(image TheatreWorks Archive, Fryer Library)

This version of the play (1988) is performed aboard a Melbourne tram as it travels from St. Kilda to the city and back. The audience ride as ordinary passengers while the characters get on and off at various stops. Although the script is written in sequential form the production is designed in such a way that conversations often occur simultaneously at different ends of the tram. Also, because the tram's speed may vary according to changing traffic flows, random events, and the propensities of different drivers, certain sequences may be extended or deleted in the course of any one trip.

## ACT ONE
## Inward Journey

*A Number 69 St. Kilda tram arrives at the St. Kilda Beach terminus in front of Luna Park. Its only passenger is* DANIEL O'ROURKE.

*He lies asleep in a dirty old overcoat, clutching an open bottle of sherry. His head is tilted sideways with one ear pressed to a transistor radio. He wears a knitted woolen cap in the colours of the Collingwood Football Club, 'The Magpies'. At his feet is a battered airline bag.*

*Understandably, people tend to avoid him as they get on.*

*They're welcomed aboard by the connie,* ALICE KATRANSKI, *who greets everyone personally, delighted to see them.*

ALICE: *[to the passengers]* Hi. Come on in. Great to see you. Welcome aboard everybody. Thanks for coming. Grab a seat. We'll get going soon.

*She helps the older folk up the step, making sure they're comfortable and that they've all got a seat. Checking their 'special' tickets as she goes round. They look like real tram tickets but have been specially printed for the play - all contain a defect that make them appear to be counterfeit - with previously clipped holes clumsily blocked in in a very clumsy attempt to make it look like the ticket hasn't already been used (which it has).*

*Eventually, when people are settled...*

ALICE: *[beaming around at them]* G'day, everybody, I'm Alice Katranski. I'm your connie for the night and I'm here to make sure you all have a wonderful time. On behalf of our Driver Tran Van Tong I'd like to welcome you aboard tram number 938: an W Class Tram travelling from St. Kilda to the City and back. Weather along the route is expected to be fine with just the possibility of a shower or two along Glenferrie Road and some turbulence outside certain pubs in South Yarra.

Our expected arrival time in Swanston Street is 9.07 pm. Thank you for travelling with the Met and just sing out if you need anything - travel sickness pills, valium, spare kimbies for the baby, that sort of thing... OK ?

*She grabs the cord about to signal the driver to start the tram.*

ALICE: So is everybody ready?

*...But she's suddenly distracted by a fit of coughing coming from DANNY's end. He wakes up and looks around to spit, is surprised to see people all around him and swallows instead. Concerned, ALICE threads her way towards him. By the time she gets there he's nodded off again.*

ALICE: [to DANNY] Excuse me, sir, we're at the terminus now. [She waits, there's no response.] You said you wanted to go to St. Kilda remember? [Shakes him] Mister ...Do you want to get off here? [He snores on.] You can't sleep there all night you know. [Still no response.] Come on mate, you're home. Time to get off. [She tries to gently lift him. He wakes with a start.]

DANNY: Hey, what are you doin'?

ALICE: Trying to help you, sir. This is where you said you wanted to go.

[He pulls back slumping into his seat again.]

DANNY: You've all been sacked. Go away.

ALICE: I beg your pardon ?

DANNY: Bloody connies, you're a waste of taxpayers' money.

ALICE: How would you know, you've never paid any taxes. *[She makes another attempt to lift him.]*

DANNY: Rack off, you're irrelevant.

*Finally* ALICE *lets him drop and for a moment just stares at him, rebuffed. Hurt. Then she nods as it slowly sinks in.*

ALICE: Oh you think so, do you ?

DANNY: Can't expect a job just cause ya got a uniform.

ALICE: *[suddenly annoyed]* So what happens if a mother with a pram wants to get on? Or someone in a wheel chair? If us connies go, who'll stop the vandals or help tourists? Who'll tell you when your stop's coming up or how you get to Malvern? You know why people feel safer on trams? 'Cause we're there to protect them. Is that what you want? More seats slashed and people too afraid to go out at night?

DANNY: Go away, you're a drain on the public purse.

ALICE: This tram isn't supposed to make a profit. It's here to provide a service. It's an investment by the people in their own means of transport. *[She turns to the rest of the passengers.]* Do you want me to go? Is that what you want?

*They respond overwhelmingly in the negative.*

ALL: NO !!!!

ALICE: OK then, let's get this tram on the rails. *[To* DANNY] Let's show him who's relevant.

*Unconcerned* DANNY *nods off again and is soon snoring.*

ALICE *pulls the cord and the tram starts moving just as* SAMANTHA HART-BYRNE *rushes up and virtually throws herself in through the doorway.*

SAM: Stop! Oh Stop! Please Stop!

*She comes on breathless and somewhat out of place in her expensive, formal evening wear.*

SAM: Is this vehicle going to Melbourne, dear?

ALICE *takes the cigarette out of* SAM's *holder.*

ALICE: I'm sorry, madam, no smoking allowed on trams.

SAM: I beg your pardon?

ALICE *points to the 'No Smoking' sign and drags the last few puffs out of SAM'S cigarette while* SAM *turns to look for the sign.*

ALICE: Don't want to ruin your health, love.

ALICE *coughs and throws the cigarette out the doorway.*

ALICE: There, see, I've just added another ten minutes to your lifespan. You'll thank me for that one day.

SAM: Oh. *[Looks around, uncertain]*

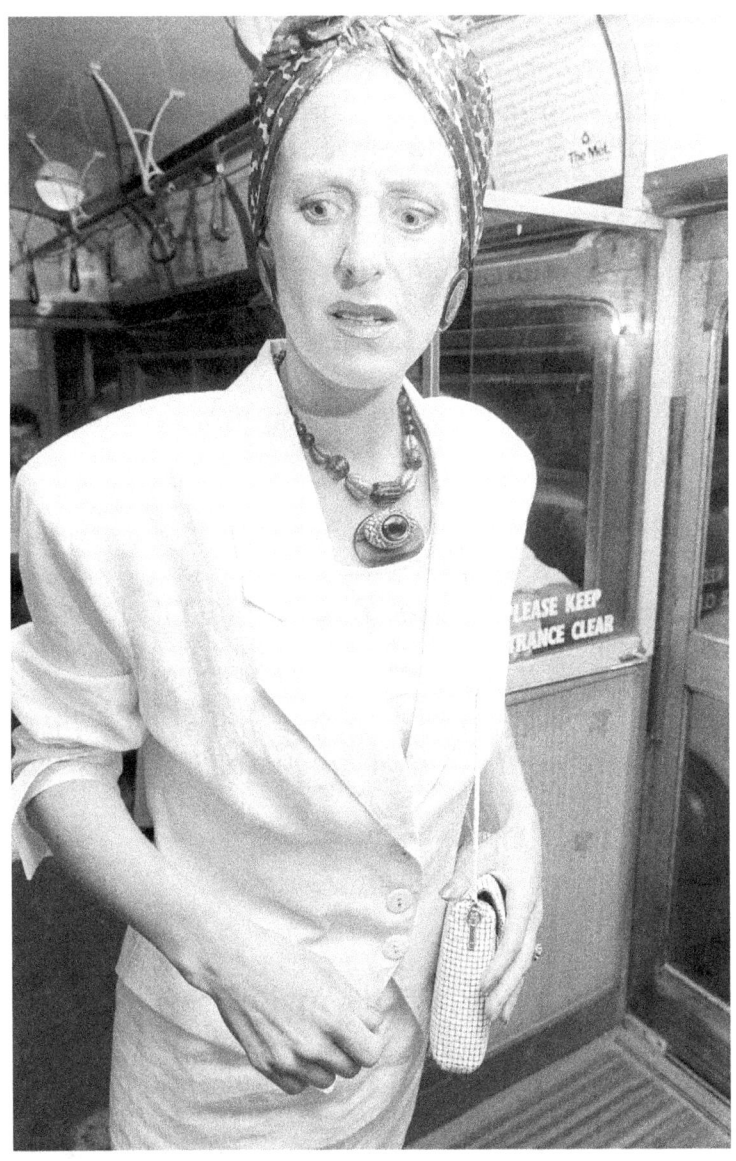

SAM: But it does go past the Arts Centre?

ALICE: Sure does.

SAM: Do you know I've been waiting twenty minutes for a cab? It's impossible to hail one. They just completely ignore you.

ALICE: We never reject anyone. Six hundred and thirty three cars on the largest tram system in the world and we'll take whoever wants to get on.

SAM: I thought if I don't jump on now I'll never get there - you know what the opera's like. *[ALICE nods blankly]* A few seconds late and you have to watch the first act on a television monitor in the foyer.

ALICE: Well, you're alright now. We'll look after you.

SAM: Do I pay you or what?

ALICE: Just take a seat and I'll he with you in a minute.

SAM *looks around at the unsavoury lot occupying all the seats and grimaces at the prospect.*

SAM: Sit anywhere?

ALICE: Sure.

SAM: But which end's first class?

ALICE: *[proudly]* It's ALL first class.

SAM: *[shocked]* Oh. Well - I'll...just pop in to the WC then and powder my nose. *[Heading for the rear driver's door]*

ALICE: Hang on, that's the driver's compartment!

SAM *hesitates, uncertain, and losing her balance, accidentally stands on* DANNY's *foot.*

*The weight of her stiletto explodes him back into life.*

DANNY: AHHHH! *[He springs forward out of his seat, dropping his tranny.]*

SAM: Oh...

DANNY *just hangs there in shock and pain, staring down at his tiny radio, trying to focus on what's actually happened.*

DANNY: Gawd, you've busted it.

*Picking his tranny up, turning it over.*

SAM: I'm sorry about that.

DANNY: *[shaking the radio next to his ear]* Fifteen quid on 'Old Rissoles' in the last at Moonee Valley and I won't even be able to hear the race. *[He drops back into his seat suddenly reminded of the acute pain in his left foot.]* Gawd, what have ya done down here? *[Tugging at his filthy old shoe - the two shoes are completely odd.]*

SAM: Look - I lost my balance. I'm afraid I'm not used to trams. *[Pressing a hankie to her nose]* Please don't take that off...

*But she's too late, he has the shoe off and is now tugging at his `sock'- a rubber glove with holes cut in the fingers to stick his toes through. He hands it to* SAM.

DANNY: Here, hold that for me will you love.

*The sock glistens with sweat. Naturally* SAMANTHA *recoils in horror and almost faints.*

DANNY: *[turning to the others, indicating the holes in his shoes]* Well, I've got to keep me foot dry haven't I?

SAM: *[escaping to the other end of the tram]* Has anyone seen a Porsche going past?

DANNY: She's definitely broken something. *[Examining the toes]* There's no feeling in the little one.

ALICE: Fares thanks.

SAM: How much is it to Melbourne dear?

ALICE: Dollar sixty and you can travel all night.

SAM: A dollar sixty! Do you take Visa?

ALICE: Sorry, madam, I can only take cash.

SAM: But I don't have any cash on me. Michael ran off in a huff and left me with the bill at Jean Jacques. It took every cent I've got just to manage the tip.

DANNY: *[fumbling in his many pockets]* Here you are, gorgeous, I'll shout ya fare for ya. Even though you've nearly crippled me for life.

SAM: I couldn't possibly...

DANNY: *[holding out a fist full of coins]* Go on take it.

SAM: Thank you but I can't accept that.

DANNY: Take the dough, f'crissake.

SAM: I couldn't possibly accept charity from someone like you.

DANNY: What's wrong with me money? It won't bite ya.

ALICE: You'll have to buy a ticket, lady, I could get into big trouble.

SAM: Oh - well... *[Reluctantly, SAM takes DANNY'S coins and hands them on to ALICE. It nearly kills her to be indebted to him.]*

DANNY: Daniel O'Rourke, Political Scientist and Turf consultant, at your service, m' lady. *[He raises his beanie. She tries to ignore him, not sure whether he's sending her up or not.]*

*The tram stops and CATHY WATERMAN gets on.*

SAM: *[taking her ticket as ALICE clips it and hands it back]* Is it always this crowded, dear?

ALICE: I'm sure some gentleman will stand up for you.

SAM: Yes. I always say good manners don't cost anything.
And they are a sign of special breeding.

DANNY: Like 'Old Rissoles'.

SAM: I beg your pardon?

DANNY: Put your pension cheque on him and you'll be laughing. *[SAMANTHA still doesn't get the racing reference]* Here, you can have my seat, alright? *[Struggles to his feet]* Just park it in there.

SAM: But I have to sit facing the way we're going.

DANNY: *[Indicating towards the rear of the tram, obviously confused about the direction it's going]* Well plonk it there and turn ya silly head sideways.

ALICE *notices* CATHY *and goes to get her ticket while* SAM *wipes the seat with her scarf, checks the scarf for stains and sits on an angle, facing forwards. Because there are no other seats left* DANNY *unfolds a camp stool and sits in the middle of the aisle. This has the effect of bringing him closer to his wounded foot.*

DANNY: Gawd strewth, I thought they were nailin' me to the flamin cross.

CATHY: *[to* ALICE *up the other end]* Pensioner concession thanks.

ALICE *baulks at this and frowns. She looks* CATHY *up and down.* CATHY's *costume hardly fits the `pensioner' stereotype. Nevertheless* ALICE *punches out a ticket somewhat dubiously.*

*Then she turns back to notice DANNY on his camp stool.*

ALICE: *[hurrying back up to him]* Oh, look, you can't sit there - you're blocking the aisle.

DANNY: *[glancing down at the narrow gap on either side]* No, I'm not.

ALICE: *[to the rest of the tram]* You see, you see why we're needed!? This is exactly the sort of thing that makes connies necessary.

DANNY: Look, I've paid me fare, I can sit anywhere I damn well like.

ALICE: You haven't paid your fare. You've been on this tram for over four hours now. And you still haven't bought a ticket.

DANNY: Four hours! Bloody slow tram! What time is it?

ALICE: *[Checking her watch]* It's half past eight.

DANNY: Half past eight *[looks around, thinks]* Would that be like, you know, half past eight in the morning or half past eight in the afternoon?

ALICE: What does it look like?

DANNY: I dunno love, it's all this daylight saving it mucks me up you know.

ALICE: Can't you see that it's dark outside!

DANNY: Not without me glasses.

ALICE: Oh! *[gives up]*

*DANNY:* Well how much longer till we get to St. Kilda?

ALICE: We've just left St. Kilda.

DANNY: Well, I want to go back.

ALICE: But you can't go back.

DANNY: I want to go back!

ALICE: *[yelling]* You can't go back!

DANNY: *[yelling]* Why not!

ALICE: Because this is a tram it doesn't *go* backwards!

DANNY: *[pointing to the front]* Well all I know is we were going backwards on the way out!

ALICE: *[pulls the cord]* Right, you're getting off.

SAM: Hear, hear.

DANNY: Look, love...

ALICE: No - I don't want to talk about it. That's it, you're out!

DANNY: Look, love, I just want to go where I paid to go, you know.

ALICE: And I really want you to go there too.

SAM: I think we all do.

ALICE: *[Indicating through the window]* So you get off at the next stop, walk across the road to the stop on the other side and you catch the next tram *back* to St. Kilda!

DANNY: *[showing his foot to her]* How can I get off if I can't even walk!

ALICE *gives up and moves away from him.*

DANNY: *[muttering on to no one in particular]* Hah! Bloody connies, don't know whether they're coming or going. Wouldn't work in an iron lung half of 'em. What on earth do we need 'em for? Should be free anyway, DANNY (cont.) public transport. Save the petrol. I reckon. Never add up the real cost of cars do they? Eh? When they close another rail line...never add up the cost of all the trucks and bridges and lead poisoning that replaces it. All the car insurance and road trauma, fatal bus smashes...No, no, they never take that into account when they say the trams are losing money.

*Half-way through the above rave* SAM *has had enough. She springs out of her seat and strides down to where* ALICE *is polishing one of the internal glass windows.*

SAM: Doesn't look like he's leaving...

ALICE: *[resignedly]* Ah well -

SAM: Yes, but don't you think you should *do* something?

ALICE: *Do* something?

SAM: Well, yes...tell the driver.

ALICE: The driver? Tran? Oh, he already knows. They had a bit of a punch up half an hour ago.

SAM: We pay enough in taxes for a decent social welfare system - you'd think there'd be somewhere he could be taken care of.

ALICE: I don't think he'd go.

SAM: Well, I'm sorry, but he's really getting on my nerves. It's not right that people should be subjected to it.

ALICE: Oh I agree.

SAM: I mean the worst thing to do is to give them money. But it just goes straight into the till at the nearest grog shop. What they really need of course is a decent meal. But you buy them a meat pie or a Chicko Roll and what happens after that you wonder?

DANNY: *[muttering over* SAM'S *spiel]* Taxes, what taxes? Her mob don't pay taxes, they pay accountants. It's poor mugs like us who pay taxes...

SAM: *[suddenly rounding on him. screaming]* Will you SHUT-UP!

DANNY: *[yelling back]* I wouldn't take ya Chicko Roll lady 'cause I'm fasting. And I'm fasting cause I'm fed up. I'm fasting till they take me where I paid to go!

SAM: *[ploughs on at* ALICE*]* I know times are tough. I know people are hurting. Michael and I tried, we really struggled to keep the second maid and the cook. But when you lose half your readies on Grey Tuesday and the rest of it in the Squatter's Friendly Society well, you can't be a charity to everyone. Michael's already sacrificed the boat and I actually went out to work. I'm not afraid to get my hands dirty. I'll muck in with the best of them. Friend of Daddy's found me a nice little possie at Channel 10 scanning movies to work out where the ads should go. Now whenever things reach an emotional climax with Michael I half expect a commercial break to occur.

DANNY: *[cutting in to the above, talking to people around him]* Well, here we all are, eh? The car-less society. People too young or too old, or too smart to drive. Too poor to afford a car. Well, put ya pension cheque on Old Rissoles in the last at Moonee Valley and you'll be laughing. *[Stops, has a thought].* Or was that yesterday? *[Pulls a crumpled racing form out of his back pocket]* Ah no. It's Friday already *[he's actually a couple of days out]* I must've skipped Thursday altogether. Christ my bloody memory. Friday already. Still, it's great isn't it? You meet a better class of person altogether on a tram.

SAM: *[again the sudden manic scream back at him]* Oh will you SHUT-UP you parasite!

DANNY: *[yelling back at her]* There's definitely something not in working order down here! *[Pointing to his foot.]*

SAM *starts to break down, her prim and proper facade crumbles.*

SAM: And now he's gone and dumped me!

ALICE: Who?

SAM: Michael. I never expected him to leave me there.

ALICE: Oh...he left you on the ahm - at the restaurant?

SAM: As if there's nothing more to say after ten years of marriage, but 'get out and good riddance.'

ALICE: *[glad of an excuse to move away, she notices* DANNY *trying to reach for the cord]* Looks like he's going at last. *[moves back to* DANNY'S *end of the tram, pulling the cord for him while* SAM *takes out her make-up and touches up her lipstick.]*
*[To DANNY]* How you feeling now?

DANNY: I'm not love, I'm not feeling at all. I'm mainly relying on taste and hearing.

ALICE: *[hopefully]* You want to get off here?

DANNY: What, in the middle of nowhere?

ALICE: Alright, but you're only getting further away from where you said you wanted to go.

DANNY: That's true of the whole world love. Yeah, that's the trouble.

*Meanwhile the tram does stop and NIGEL DAVIDSON gets on. He wears sunglasses, expensive casual clothes and carries a leather briefcase. He drops into an empty seat and takes out a small tape recorder, speaking into it.*

NIGEL: Scene two. Interior Tram, full stop. He blew in from a street blacker than hell and sat near the door. It was Melbourne alright. He could tell from the vacant stares and the empty minds of the hideous faces all around him. Melbourne faces trapped in a Melbourne gloom. Pimply masks that stared back at him pleading for answers to the really big questions like: Where are we going? When will we get there? How much will it cost? Have I left the stove on?

*He only gradually becomes aware of ALICE standing above him.*

ALICE: Fares thanks.

NIGEL: *[He takes a flower out of his button hole and wraps a $5 note around it, handing it to her, then continues talking into his recorder]* He took a red flower out of his button hole and handed it to her saying, 'That's to match the perfume of your loveliness.' That's to match the perfume of you loveliness.

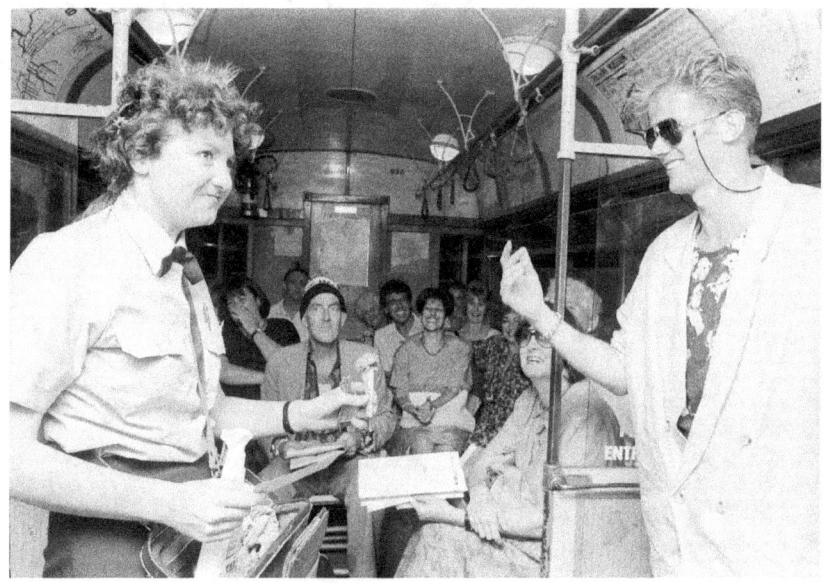

ALICE, *lost for words, hunts for change.*

NIGEL: Please, keep the change.
=
ALICE: Thanks.

ALICE *smiles, chuffed, confused, unsure, puts the flower in her button hole. Up the other end,* SAM *has been chewing over the last few minutes and probably over the last few years of her life. She comes up and zeros in on* ALICE *again.*

SAM: I just wanted you to know that I'm not utterly dependent on Michael.

ALICE *is beginning to really wish she'd go away.*

ALICE: Oh good...

SAM: I've always prided myself on that. I've never been utterly dependent on anyone.

ALICE: Uh huh.

SAM: He even accused me once of being trendy.

ALICE: *[sympathetic]* Ah -

DANNY: *[from down the back]* That must've been a long time ago, love.

SAM *stabs a venomous look at him, but chooses to ignore the remark.*

SAM: You know, my dear, I am not, repeat not trendy. I loathe trendy people. I mean, all the trendies left our gym ages ago.

ALICE: Right. [ALICE *moves away, but* SAM *follows.]*

NIGEL: *[into tape recorder, watching* SAM *move off]* She talked about a husband from no-man's land. A wicked butterfly with shoulder pads like exploding volcanoes. Was he alive, or just in Caulfield?

*But NIGEL gets bored with the tape, the dialogue just isn't flowing. Instead he takes out a small camera and holds it out to take shots of himself in the window. NIGEL completely fails to notice CATHY sitting a few seats away, also listening in.*

SAM: *[to ALICE] It's* quite inhuman. He expects me to be perfect. The perfect wife, the perfect cook, the perfect hostess, and oh yes, his mother can do it. But she's got help! I don't of course - now. I don't have help! Since the crash happened Michael thinks that's just too bourgeois. We can't afford it. But I told him in the car tonight, I said, `Michael, I need **HELP!**'

DANNY: That's an understatement.

ALICE: And he didn't accept that?

SAM: He laughed. He tossed back his Terence Marini hairdo and giggled like the gormless twerp that he is. He said `You've got Mrs. White to do the ironing, what more do you want?' I saw then just how ugly he was.

ALICE: Oh -

SAM: Because, of course, when you're married to Michael you're not supposed to *do* anything. You're supposed to stay at home and be there for him when he has to bring a client back, or needs an escort to the opera. I get so bored with shopping, I'm sick of watching soap operas, and there's only so much time one can spend gossiping to the hairdresser.

ALICE: Why don't you tell him how you feel?

SAM: Oh, I intend to, I intend to make it perfectly clear. The next time he asks me to throw a dinner party I'm going to throw one alright. I'm going to throw it all over him.

ALICE: Gee.

SAM: The last time I complained about losing domestic staff he threw Cynthia Montstephen up as some kind of example.

DANNY: I'd regurgitate her myself.

SAM: It's pathetic, really, she's so trivial she even went on 'Sale Of The Century.'

ALICE: Oh - did she win anything?

SAM: The Franco Cozzo furniture. I can see it fitting in perfectly with their Surfers penthouse. New money has nothing but a bad effect on people. You've only got to look at Michael. I thought I'd rather catch a cab than travel another inch with him. And I'm blowed if he's getting away with it. No. I'm going to the opera under my own steam and I'm going to tell him exactly how I feel.

ALICE: Good for you, love. That's the spirit.

*Meanwhile, bored with his own self-image,* NIGEL *has started taking various shots around the tram of other people and suddenly notices* CATHY *through his view finder down the back. Uncertain, he moves tentatively towards her.*

NIGEL: *[to* CATHY*]* Look, I know this sounds corny, but, haven't I seen you somewhere before?

CATHY: Get real Nigel, we had a permanent relationship eleven years ago.

NIGEL *is shocked, thrown by a torrent of memories that come flooding back.*

NIGEL: Cathy? Cathy Waterman? Oh Wow! This is incredible.
*[Nodding, amazed]* Hey - how are you?

CATHY: I'm O.K...better.

NIGEL: You look great, great shape.

CATHY: Yeah, I'm alright. My neck still gives me a bit of trouble.

NIGEL: Your neck? Your neck is still giving you trouble?

CATHY: Yeah, so how are you?

NIGEL: Your neck? You're saying that time I threw the...

CATHY: Yes, it still hurts. How are you?

NIGEL: I'm fine, you know...surviving. Gosh I can't believe that it still ...after all this time, it still hurts.

CATHY: Don't worry about it.

NIGEL: Yeah, but god...

CATHY: I heard you ended up in Sydney.

NIGEL: Yeah, well...'ended' no. Hell I'm just beginning. My career is really taking off.

CATHY: Again?

NIGEL: Yeah...No. What do you mean again?

CATHY: You were going to make the great Australian film, remember?

NIGEL: *[painful memory]* Oh yeah, that. Well *[shrugs]* someday.

CATHY: On Super 8.

NIGEL: You can't buy Super 8 anymore.

CATHY: So - what are you doing, now?

NIGEL: Oh, mmm...tapes mostly.

CATHY: What sort of tapes?

NIGEL: And some theatre.

CATHY: Really.

NIGEL: Business theatre.

CATHY: What?

NIGEL: Product launches. You know, we have the product on stage and then I organise the dancers and the band, and we usually have a comic these days, a stand-up character you know, and...and the design is really big. The lighting budget alone...

CATHY: You're in advertising.

NIGEL: Corporate Promotion.

CATHY: Oh Nigel -

NIGEL: Come on it's really big these days. John Cleese did it.

CATHY: You've sold out, Nigel.

NIGEL: It's a living.

CATHY: It's a lie.

NIGEL: God, is it thirteen years?

CATHY: Eleven years.

NIGEL: Quite a while.

CATHY: Yeah, I haven't been repelled by anybody like this for ages.

NIGEL: *[astounded]* What, are you kidding? Repelled!? After a dozen years you're still repelled by me? I'm suffering here Cathy, that really hurts you know.

CATHY: Time wounds all heels, Nigel.

NIGEL: What an amazing coincidence.

CATHY: Yeah, amazing.

NIGEL: So... are you...what - still living here or something, still living in Melbourne?

CATHY: Balaclava actually.

NIGEL: Balaclava!

CATHY: I like the trees, I like the fact you can catch a tram to the beach.

NIGEL: Did I say something?

CATHY: No, you said nothing, Nigel, nothing for eleven years.

NIGEL. OK, OK, *I...[shrugs, lost]*

CATHY: You haven't changed much.

NIGEL: You'd be amazed at how different I am.

CATHY: I know your biro doesn't work.

NIGEL: How did I know where you'd gone forgodsake!

CATHY: You're the one who left, Nigel, all you had to do was ask.

NIGEL: Well it cuts both ways, hon, you didn't write to me either.

CATHY: What on earth was there to say?

NIGEL: God you're cynical.

CATHY: No, Nigel, just a little older and a lot wiser and a great deal more experienced.

NIGEL: Wiser huh? That why you're buried out here in the great suburban stupor. Whatever happened to Brunswick Street?

CATHY: I got sick of red falcons and laminex and people who looked like they'd just stepped out of a Pepsi ad.

NIGEL: Yeah, I suppose this *is* Melbourne.

CATHY: I like Melbourne, at least in Melbourne people think.

NIGEL: No, they only think they think.

CATHY: Nigel, I know Sydney it's all form and no content. I can *see* why it suits you.

NIGEL: Sixty percent of people living in Melbourne actually wish they were somewhere else. Did you know that? [CATHY *groans.*] Do you realise what that says about the place.?

CATHY: So I enjoy being in a minority.

NIGEL: I mean, live in Melbourne 800 billion flies can't be wrong.

CATHY *picks up her bag and moves away from him.*

NIGEL: The only time I ever hear about Sydney is when I come to Melbourne.

NIGEL *just hangs there in shock. No one's walked out on him like this for ages. After some moments of thinking about it he picks up his brief case and follows her. On the way he passes* DANNY.

DANNY: *[to* SAM] You wouldn't have the time would you love? [SAM *ignores him.]* Excuse me, love...

SAM: *[snaps]* I don't have a watch!

DANNY: Perhaps I could interest you in one. *[Rolling back a sleeve - exposing an armful of watches]* Men's? Ladies? Digital?

SAM: No thank you.

DANNY: Solar powered?

SAM: I said No!

DANNY: Fully guaranteed.

SAM: Will you please go away.

DANNY: *[turning to another passenger]* What about you, mate? How about ten quid for the black one, it was going only yesterday. *[He doesn't have much luck.]* Well what about a transistor radio? *[Pulling out his radio, shaking it]* Made in Japan. Works beautifully. *[DANNY switches it on, gets a lot of static.]* Just that on the tram with all the wires, you know. *[Goes on to another passenger]* 'Scuse me mate, wouldn't have the time would you?

*While* DANNY *tries to sell watches,* NIGEL *comes back to* CATHY, *contrite.*

NIGEL: Look I went to Sydney because I needed a change...needed *to* change.

CATHY: Yeah, yeah, I've heard it all before Nigel.

NIGEL: I wanted to give you a chance to work it out.

CATHY: Oh, that was big of you.

NIGEL: Look, I admit I behaved badly, you know, point taken. But you've got to admit you were blocking, Cathy, you were really brick walling back there in Fitzroy.

CATHY: Is that your account of it? After all this time? I was 'blocking?' Where'd you pick that up, some Pyramid selling workshop?

NIGEL: There was this correspondence course in group therapy.

CATHY: "Grope" therapy more like it.

NIGEL: You don't believe I've changed, do you?

CATHY: Does water flow upstream? Is the earth flat?

NIGEL: Confidentially, Cathy, I've been...undergoing analysis.

CATHY: Yes, I thought eventually you'd have to pay people
to listen to you.

NIGEL: I've learned how to yell, Cathy.

CATHY: Eleven years later you're still trying to figure out whether your insanity is real or just a figment of your imagination?

NIGEL: The breakthrough for me was scream therapy.

CATHY: Oh, no!

NIGEL: It's a very cleansing experience. It releases the pain. You should give it a go.

CATHY: Nigel, I don't need cleansing.

NIGEL: Go on, try it.

CATHY: Nigel, please, people are listening.

NIGEL: Just grab a lung-full and let go.

CATHY: I have no intention of making a complete fool of myself in public, thank you.

NIGEL, Don't thank me 'til you've tried it.

CATHY: No! Nigel. Please! *[She makes a determined move*
*away from him again]*

NIGEL: The only way out is up, Cathy.

CATHY: The only way out is through that door and I really wish you'd take it.

NIGEL: I'll show you.

CATHY: Nigel, don't do it!

NIGEL *throws back his head and lets out a tremendous yell.* DANNY *gets an equally enormous shock and echoes the yell. He is on his feet clutching his chest when* ALICE *looks up from sweeping under some passenger's feet.*

ALICE: Who did that?

ALICE: Who made that noise? *[She looks from one passenger to another, decides* DANNY *is the most likely culprit and strides determinedly up to him.]* You think it's smart yelling out like that?

DANNY: Like what?

ALICE: You've been nothing but trouble since you got on this tram. Now I'm warning you, you'll have Tran back out here again, and he mightn't be an airline pilot but he's got the same responsibility.

DANNY: Strewth!

ALICE: Your life is his responsibility. And mine.

DANNY: I didn't do anything.

ALICE: I'm warning you, one more incident and you're off.

SAM: He's off alright.

DANNY: Geeze, what is this? Nazi Germany or something?

ALICE *goes back to her cleaning, Nigel sucks in some quick breaths*

DANNY: *[when she's safely gone]* Driver, hah! Man obviously suffers from parallelotosis. Too much staring at tram tracks. Sends 'em mad. She's got a touch of it too I'd say.

ALICE: I heard that!

DANNY: *[back at her]* Parallelotosis. Hah! You can hypnotise a chook with a straight line.

ALICE *just ignores him, while at the other end* NIGEL *comes out of his post-scream warm down.*

NIGEL: it's like birth, it's death, it's like being born and dying at the same time.

CATHY: Psychobabble.

NIGEL: What?

CATHY: How did I ever spend five years with you?

NIGEL: The kooris could kill someone with a scream like that.

CATHY: You're lucky I didn't kill you.

NIGEL: You can't censor your emotions, Cathy.

CATHY: Nigel, it's pretty obvious to me that you've landed in a scene where in order to appear interesting you've got to *be* neurotic.

NIGEL: At least I *am* interesting. I mean what are you doing out here in hills-hoist land?

CATHY: You don't do much with two kids.

NIGEL: *[shocked]* Two kids? I didn't know that.

CATHY: No, well you didn't write, did you?

NIGEL: Two kids.

CATHY: Boys unfortunately.

NIGEL: I can understand maybe, one - maybe. I mean one
kid's a work of art but two kids is a family, Cathy. What are you tying yourself down for?

CATHY: These things happen, Nigel. Life is a miracle.

NIGEL: You mean they were unplanned?

CATHY: *[again becoming acutely aware of the people listening]* I'd really like to talk about it some other time if you don't mind.

NIGEL: How old?

CATHY: Darryl's just turned ten and Morrey's eight.

NIGEL: *[doing some sums]* Just turned ten.

CATHY: Yes ten.

NIGEL: Just ten.

CATHY: Three months ago.

NIGEL: You mean nine months after I left?

CATHY: Something like that.

NIGEL: You're kidding! *[He stares at her hoping for a moment that it's all a bad dream.]* Who, ah, who's the lucky guy?

CATHY: Who do you reckon?

NIGEL: Eleven years later I get on a tram and you tell me I'm a FATHER?

CATHY: Jesus, Nigel, keep your voice down.

NIGEL: Am I a father?

CATHY: It's no big deal believe me.

NIGEL: *[breathing hard, pacing up and down]* I'm going to need another primal.

CATHY: Nigel, please don't scream again.

NIGEL: If I don't let go it can scar.

CATHY: If you do let go I'll make sure you're scarred. Just settle down and do your breathing exercises.

NIGEL: Yes, yes, breathing...breathing exercises. *[Nigel continues to pace, almost hyperventilating.]*

DANNY: That's better.

NIGEL: Two kids? Well, they're not both mine, are they? You can't pin that one on me.

CATHY: They're kids, Nigel, not medals.

NIGEL: Well, they're not both mine.

CATHY: No thank god. The youngest one's Johnno's... [trifle *embarrassed]* we had a sort of relationship for a while - after you left.

NIGEL: You're kidding! You and Johnno?!

DANNY: Who's Johnno?

NIGEL: *[contemptuous]* He's a real estate agent!

CATHY: At least he knew what day of the week the rubbish got put out.

DANNY: That's important.

NIGEL: I must be dreaming. This is worse than being nominated for a Green Room Award. Pinch me. I'm going to wake up in a minute.

CATHY: Look, I happen to actually like Johnno, do you mind?

NIGEL: There's no accounting for taste.

CATHY: He helps me out.

NIGEL: He can afford to.

CATHY: You try living on the supporting parent's benefit, see how far you'd go.

NIGEL: You don't live with him?

CATHY: We can't can we, we'd lose $207 a week.

NIGEL: Forgodsake, he sells mansions in Toorak! I know he has a cellular phone.

CATHY: I'm sorry but I don't really want to talk about this in public.

NIGEL: Oh, well yes, we'll just postpone it shall we? Put it all off till another time?

CATHY *just turns away, ignoring him.*

NIGEL: Like the flat we were going to get. *[Again no response from* CATHY.] Cathy, how can we solve this if we don't talk about it?

DANNY: Talk about it, talk about it.

CATHY: Stop projecting your self-loathing onto me.

NIGEL: Right, right, now you're getting the hang of it. Self-loathing, that's good.

CATHY: I am not like you, I am NOT NEUROTIC.

NIGEL: Not, neurotic, huh? Then how come you're dressed up like that?

CATHY: Like what?

NIGEL: Like some...Tasmanian barmaid.

CATHY: I'm going to work.

NIGEL: Work, where?

CATHY: *Tickles*.

NIGEL: *Tickles*?

CATHY: It's a Bath House.

NIGEL: What are you now a towel monitor or something?

CATHY: How else do you think I could get the fees?

NIGEL: Fees? For what?

CATHY: I'm sending Darryl and Morrey to Pious College.

NIGEL: *[disgusted]* Pious College? My son's mother is on the game so he can go to some ruling class torture chamber?

DANNY: You poor bugger.

CATHY: I'm trying to save him from a life like yours.

NIGEL: You'll turn him into a complete twit. How will he relate to me?

DANNY: Twit to twit?

CATHY: I think we should spare him the shock, don't you?

NIGEL: Aren't you at least going to let me see the kid?

CATHY: Why upset him?

NIGEL: Where is he now?

CATHY: At home with mum.

NIGEL: Your MOTHER! *[Rising panic]* She's living here too?

CATHY: She moved down from Toowoomba about eight months ago.

*Unable to contain himself* NIGEL *rushes to a door and lets out another blood curdling yell.*

NIGEL: Your MOTHAAAAAAAHHH!

CATHY: God you're a fool.

CATHY *moves down to the opposite end of the tram. Again,* ALICE *missed it because she was on her knees cleaning. She jumps up and goes straight for* DANNY.

ALICE: Was that you again?

DANNY: Who, me?

ALICE: I warned you about disturbing people.

DANNY: I haven't done anything.

ALICE: *[seizing his bottle of sherry]* What's this you've got?

DANNY: It's me cough medicine.

ALICE: Well I'm confiscating it. *[She pulls at it, he tugs back]*

DANNY: Hey, hang on.

ALICE: You're not allowed to drink on trams.

DANNY: Just my luck to cop a Presbyterian connie.

ALICE: Let go! *[He lets go and* ALICE *falls back into* SAMANTHA]

DANNY: Alright, alright, take me medicine. Shove it in ya pouch, kanga. Just don't ask me what happens when this cough turns into pneumonia.

SAM: How soon do you think you could manage that?

DANNY: Geeze lady I wouldn't want you to do me any favours.

ALICE: You want to stay on this tram you buy a ticket!

DANNY: I bought a ticket off you before.

ALICE: *[indicating* SAM] For her.

DANNY: Yeah?

ALICE: If an inspector gets on its more than my job is worth.

SAM: I think you should throw him off now. I'm sure some of the passengers will give you a hand.

DANNY: I can't love, I can't do a ticket cause I can't scratch can I? Look at me fingernails. How am I supposed to scratch a scratchie with them?

SAM: What do you do with all the lice then?

ALICE: You can use a coin.

DANNY: I don't have any coins, they all went on her ticket.

SAM: If you don't pay your fare you're a thief. You're stealing from the rest of these good people who do the right thing.

DANNY: Me, stealing? That's rich coming from a parasite like you, eating in Jean Jacques and cantering off to the opera. You're only able to do that cause you've ripped off your workers. All property is theft!

ALICE: *[to* SAM, *reaching for the cord]* Don't worry madam, he's getting off at the next stop.

DANNY: *[hopping on one foot, tugging at his other shoe]* Alright, alright, I'm down to me last quid then am I? Is that what you want? Take a poor old pensioner's last pound note.

SAM: *[Covering her nose with a scarf]* Oh please don't take that off.

DANNY: *[extracting an obsolete pound note from his shoe]* There you go then. That's sure to put a big hole in the national debt.

ALICE: *[exasperated]* We can't take pounds!

DANNY: I've had this since the Royal Visit in 1954.

ALICE: It's not legal tender.

DANNY: Look, see, same Queen - only younger.

ALICE: I'm not taking it.

DANNY: Won't take a quid, you're sick you realise that?

SAM: She's only doing her job forgoodness sake.

DANNY: And you, lady, ought to be *destroyed*.

SAMANTHA *recoils and turns away, still pressing her hankie to her nose.*

ALICE: Either you buy a ticket or I'm calling an inspector.

DANNY: Is this why I fought in the war is it? Gave my all and sacrificed everything just to be chucked off the tram like so much rubbish. These hands killed three people.[He *holds up two fingers.*]

ALICE: Yeah, I know, you were a cook in the catering corps you poisoned them.

DANNY: Very funny.

*While* DANNY *mutters on to nobody in particular* SAM *draws* ALICE *aside, away from him.*

DANNY: It's the Electromagnetic Radiation that stuffs them up you know. All that current going through the wires up there. Has a detrimental effect on the brain. Should never have gotten rid of the cable cars I reckon. Trouble is they brought all the riff raff to St. Kilda. All the rubbish from Carlton and Fitzroy. That was the beginning of the end for the place. Never been the same since. Cable cars. They're a fantastic attraction for San Francisco aren't they? You see a different sort of world from a cable car. That's like what we are: tourists, tourists in our own home town. Bring back the cable cars I say and the horse drawn tram. Save on power then, and get a bit of fertiliser going on the side. Horse drawn trams - run the whole bloody thing on grass. No need for connies then, thank god. I mean, look, look at it. You put 'em in a uniform and the power goes to their head - where it's all churned up by the wires, the electromagnetic radiation. What with that and paralellotosis, it's a wonder they've got the brain power to walk, let alone hassle poor old burnt out diggers who gave their all for their country...

*Meanwhile, at the same time, up the other end of the tram* SAM *bores in on* ALICE.

SAM: Don't you think you should phone the police?

ALICE: We don't have radios on the old trams.

SAM: I'm sorry but I think it's criminal that a young girl should be subjected to it. Does your mother know the kind of danger you face?

ALICE: Oh it's all part of the job, I don't mind, it's why we're here.

SAM: But does she know?

ALICE: I haven't actually seen Mum for four years.

SAM: Four years!

ALICE: She's been in Fairlea,

SAM: *[brightly]* Oh that's nice, where's that?

ALICE: Prison.

SAM: Oh...

*The tram stops again and* TERRY *rushes on, carrying a large plastic guide dog used for collecting money for the blind, a broken security chain dangles from round its neck.*

TERRY: *[pulling the cord urgently]* Come on let's go let's get out of here.

*As soon the tram moves off he laughs, and gives the fingers to his pursuers, confident now that he's gotten away with it. He looks quite intimidating with his bright, mad staring eyes, luminous hair, body piercing and crazy outfit. He turns to someone nearby*

TERRY: Wanna give a little puppy some spare coins?

SAM *though is appalled at what he's obviously done, and rounds on him, unable to restrain herself.*

SAM: Wherever did you get that?

TERRY: Get wot?

SAM: That dog, you've stolen it.

TERRY: *[looks around at the dog and leaps back in mock fright]* Ah!

SAM: You've taken that dog from its rightful owners.

TERRY: What makes you say that, lady?

SAM *hesitates as she takes in his black lipstick, backs off a little. And while* TERRY *focuses on* SAM, DANNY *becomes interested in the dog and the money it holds.*

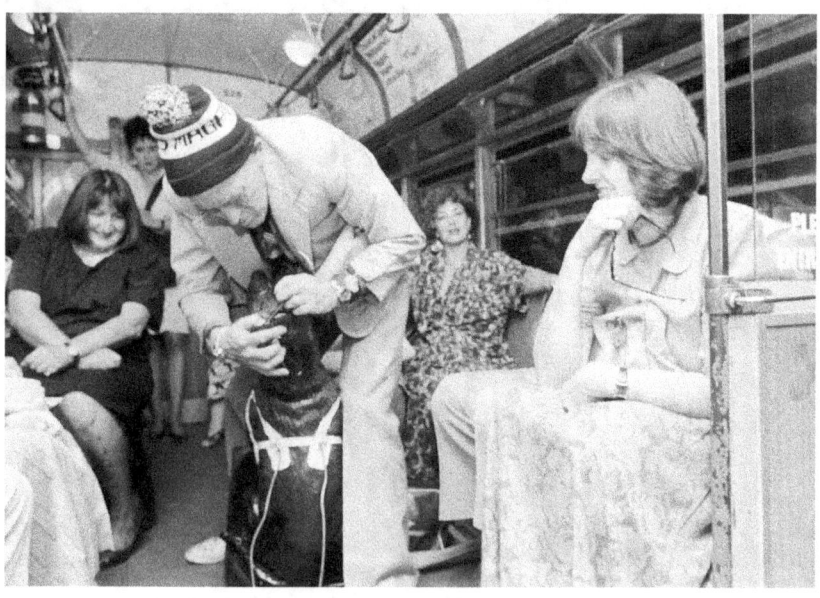

SAM: I've worked for the blind society and I know that they certainly wouldn't give a dog like that to somebody like you.

TERRY: Whaddayew mean somebody like me?

SAM: *[looking him up and down]* Somebody like you.

TERRY: Yeah, so?

SAM: *[backing off]* So...

TERRY: So he followed me here, didn't he?

SAM: But that's ridiculous, he can't even walk.

TERRY: No...he can't *see*, that's why I'm taking him home.

SAM: What are you rebelling against?

TERRY: What 'a ya got?

*She continues backing away from* TERRY, *unsure of her ground now, he bores in on her forcing her back while down the other end* DANNY *is trying to entice the dog with a dry biscuit.*

SAM: Is it part of the cult to wear your hair like that? I mean, why all the black? Are you in mourning or something? Has someone just died in your family?

TERRY: Yeah, me dad...

SAM: [suddenly sympathetic] Oh...

TERRY: I just topped him with a chainsaw out in Broady.

*Since that's obviously rubbish* SAM *barrels on.*

SAM: No, no, I am interested - from a sociological point of view...you *see I* did an essay once at La Trobe...on social deviates...

TERRY: Oh ya studying me are ya, love?

SAM: No, no really, ah...

TERRY: Well this is what we do - *[starts embracing her]*

SAM: *[screams and leaps back]* Stop it, stop it! How dare you! I can't bear to be handled by someone I haven't been introduced to!

TERRY: The name's 'Mickey Mouse', love, what's yours?

SAM: Samantha Hart-Byrne, and I know that dogs are not allowed on trams.

TERRY: *[mock hurt]* Oh don't listen, Bozo... *[he glances round just as DANNY tips the dog upside down to shake out some coins.]* Hey, derro! *[DANNY freezes.]*
Whaddayew think you're doin'?

DANNY: I was just trying to teach him a back flip.

TERRY: *[wrenching the dog back]* I know you. You're the warm patch pervert.

DANNY: The what?

TERRY: *[to the tram generally]* He gets a big thrill from sliding onto a seat just after someone's left it. Feeling the warmth of their bodies on his botty.

DANNY: I do not.

TERRY: Slimey old pervert.

DANNY: That's rubbish.

TERRY: *[grabbing him in an armlock and rummaging through his pockets]* Ought to be locked up if you ask me.

DANNY: Hey, I had a few quid in there.

TERRY: Poo, you smell like toilet.

DANNY: Get out of it, ya young thug.

TERRY: Had a few drinks have ya mate?

DANNY: Let go.

TERRY: Had a few drinks with ya mates after work?

DANNY: I don't work, I think.

TERRY: Course you do, it's dribbled all over ya. See...

TERRY *Points at some congealed food on* DANNY'S *coat lapel.* DANNY *looks down and* TERRY *flicks his nose with the pointing finger. An old trick.* TERRY *laughs.*

DANNY: Ah you bastard! *[Reeling back holding his nose]*

ALICE *summons enough courage to finally intervene.*

ALICE: Fares thanks.

TERRY *does a slow, exaggerated turn, and his eyes light up as he takes* ALICE *in from head to foot.*

TERRY: *[ecstatic]* Oh, you...are...be-u-ti-ful.

ALICE: Yeah, and you're Mr. Universe, big deal, so show me your ticket or buy another one.

TERRY: I LOVE you!

ALICE: Then you won't mind handing me some money will you?

TERRY: How much *are* you, love?

ALICE: It's $1.60 for three hours.

TERRY: Gee you're cheap.

ALICE: *[slaps him]* How dare you!

TERRY *rolls his eyes dizzily and reels back as if punch drunk.*

TERRY: Oh I *love* it when you do that! *[Notices* DANNY *fiddling with his radio]* Hey, derro, get something romantic on that thing, I think I'm falling in love.

TERRY *grabs the radio and finds some music.*

DANNY: It works!

TERRY *starts gyrating to the music moving seductively in on* ALICE.

ALICE: Don't push it, mate, I've been hassled by experts.

TERRY: What's wrong with ya, don't you like dancing?

DANNY: *[pointing at his hair]* Hey, mate, you didn't stick ya finger in a light plug did ya, and switch it on? *[Laughs]*

TERRY *ignores him, continues to gyrate in front of* ALICE.

ALICE: Do you want me to call the driver?

TERRY: Got a scene with him or something?

ALICE: I'm warning you, I've had it up to here and I'm not going to take it anymore.

TERRY: Geeze, if ya don't like your job mate, why don-cha just chuck it in.

ALICE: I like my job. It's YOU that's the problem. You're ruining it for everybody. *[Grabs the radio from* TERRY, *switches it off.]* People like you, just don't care do you? Well I do. I care about this job. I care about public transport. And I'm damned if I'm going to see people turned off it because of idiots like you. You think you're smart, well, you're not, you're embarrassing. It's pathetic, why don't you grow up?

*The tram stops and Terry notices* DANNY *unscrewing the bottom of the dog to extract more coins.*

TERRY: *[charging right up to him]* Hey, I thought I told you to leave Bozo alone.

DANNY: Well you took my radio.

TERRY: Wot? This radio? *[Takes it off him again.]*

DANNY: *[reaching for it]* Yeah.

TERRY: *[holding it high, away from DANNY]* Does it bounce? If I chuck it out the window?

DANNY: Give it back. I'm missing the fourth race.

TERRY: OK. *[Gives it back]* No hard feelings. *[Holding out his hand]* Shake.

DANNY, *tentative, takes his hand, then writhes in pain as* TERRY *squeezes hard.*

DANNY: Oooh, ahh! ya squashin all me knuckles.

TERRY: That's cause I've got a firm personality.

DANNY: *[trying to extricate his hand from TERRY'S grip]* Stuff off ya mongrel.

TERRY: What? *[Suddenly serious]*

DANNY: *[finally pulling his hand free]* I said stuff off!

TERRY: We'll have no bad language on this tram thank you very much. *[Grabbing DANNY'S arm, pushing him towards the open door]*

DANNY: Get out of it.

TERRY: I don't think you deserve a free ride *[pushing DANNY towards the door]*.

DANNY: Hey, hang on.

TERRY: You heard the lady, she doesn't want nobody messing up the transport.

DANNY: What are you doing you young lunatic?

*The tram stops again, the door opens and clutching DANNY by the seat of the pants, TERRY frog marches him straight out through it.*

TERRY: Bye Bye Grandpa!

DANNY: *[trying to grab onto the hand rail]* I want to go to St. Kilda!

TERRY: Well off you go then. There's Punt Road, start walkin'.

*And in one swift movement TERRY shoves DANNY completely out the door. Before DANNY can recover his balance out on the road the door closes and the tram moves off again.*

DANNY: *[off]* Hey! *[Running along outside, banging on the door.]* Hey! Stop! Hey you bloody animal! You punk fascist bastard!!

TERRY: *[Waving back laughing]* Come on grandpa! Lift those knees, only joggers die young! Smelly old coot. You'll probably make the next Olympics.

DANNY'S *howls of protest fade off behind the tram as he disappears behind it into the night.*

TERRY: *[turning back to ALICE]* There you are love, nice quiet tram for you.

ALICE *just shakes her head at him and turns away.*

NIGEL *passes* TERRY *en route back up to* CATHY.

NIGEL: *[to* CATHY] I just want...

CATHY: No, Nigel.

NIGEL: ...to ask you a question. Are men and women - is there something fundamentally different?

CATHY: Oh Nigel please don't go into that again.

NIGEL: No, really, do our brains function differently? As differently as our bodies?

CATHY: Jesus!

NIGEL: Because they must. It stands to reason, our bodies ARE different.

CATHY: If you go on like this I AM going to scream.

NIGEL: I'm sorry...it's just such a shock.

CATHY: *[relenting]* I suppose it's not everyday you find out you're a father.

NIGEL: No, I mean the thought of you doing it for money.

CATHY: Nigel, I don't have any skills. How else can I earn good money? I'm not perfect, I never said I was.

NIGEL: It's just that I feel so...guilty.

CATHY: If you're going to go on about it, I'm getting off right now.

NIGEL: Come with me...?

CATHY: No.

NIGEL: Come on, just for old time's sake. We'll always have Brunswick.

CATHY: Thanks for reminding me. I'd been trying to forget.

NIGEL: Look - just have a drink with me. Just one drink. A coffee, cocktail, whatever you want... I just...want to know about Derryn.

CATHY: Darryl.

NIGEL: Yeah. What sort of bands does he listen to, what movies does he like? Is he incredibly good looking...I mean what have you told him about me? Does he even know I exist?

CATHY: I told him you were a crusading journalist who had disappeared in South America.

NIGEL: South America? Why South America?

CATHY: I was trying to say you'd gone into oblivion, it just came out as Bolivia.

NIGEL: So he thinks I'm a hero? Cathy, I'm moved.

CATHY: I told him you were a selfless, brave, intelligent, sane, generous, caring, sharing human being.

NIGEL: You told him that! You mean I have to live up to that?

CATHY: You were always good at faking it, Nigel.

NIGEL: Don't walk out on me now, Cathy, I've GOT to know more.

CATHY: I'm going to work.

NIGEL: Work! Is that what you call it?

CATHY: Yes, work!

NIGEL: OK - I'm loose about it.

CATHY: Good.

NIGEL: You're loose about it - I'm loose about it.

CATHY: Good.

NIGEL: You *are* - loose about it?

CATHY: Yes, I'm loose.

TERRY: She must be a loose woman.

TERRY *laughs,* ALICE *hits him, he continues to hang off a handrail, conspicuously listening in to* NIGEL *and* CATHY, *sending them up behind their backs.*

NIGEL: *[opening his wallet]* Look, I'll pay you for your time.

CATHY: NO you won't.

NIGEL: I don't expect any favours, Cathy.

CATHY: Nigel, you couldn't possibly afford it.

NIGEL: *[pulling out a couple of twenty dollar bills]* How much?

CATHY: Two hundred and fifty.

NIGEL: *[staggered]* A night!

CATHY: An hour.

NIGEL'S *jaw drops, the tram stops and* CATHY *picks up her bag to leave.* NIGEL *meekly follows, passing* MORRIS STANLEY *as he gets on.*

NIGEL: *[as they exit]* Couldn't you ring in sick or something?

CATHY: We don't get sick pay.

NIGEL: *[hovering around her on the footpath]* You're piloting out on me, Cathy.

CATHY: Oh god!

NIGEL: I mean, Geezus, I love you forgodsake. There's a lot to talk about.

CATHY: There's nothing to talk about, Nigel it's 1988.

NIGEL: Twelve years till the end of the millennium. People will soon be living on Mars!

CATHY: I wish you were living on Mars.

NIGEL: Well, look, just talk to you as we walk along, OK?

CATHY: You've got fifteen minutes, Nigel.

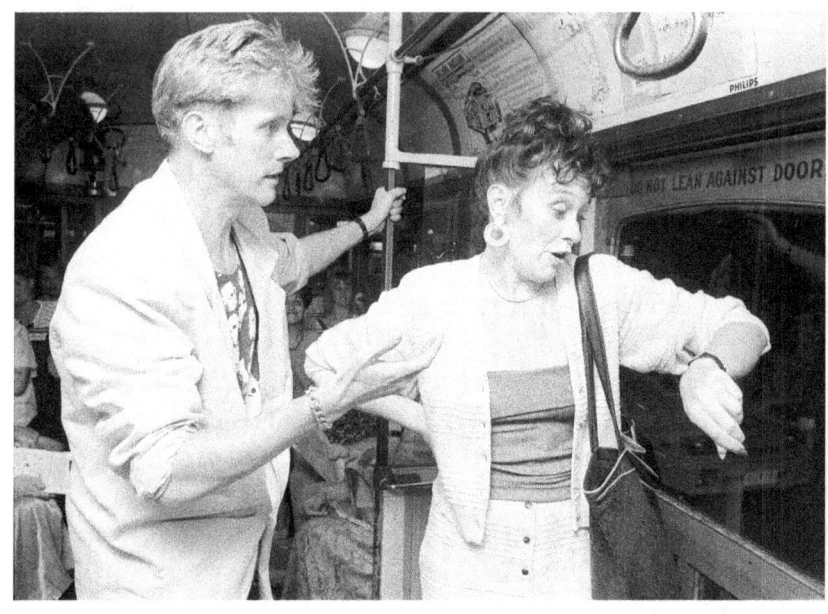

NIGEL: *[pleading]* Twenty minutes, twenty minutes.

CATHY: *[checking her watch]* Fourteen minutes.

NIGEL: You're putting a stopwatch on this now? It's been thirteen years!

CATHY: Eleven years.

NIGEL: A dog's entire lifetime.

CATHY: I knew this was going to be a shocking day...

*Their conversation fades out as the tram moves on... Meanwhile MORRIS STANLEY, in his trench coat, pork pie hat stands commandingly near the doorway where he got on. He stabs a quick glance round at the passengers, his eyes narrowing with suspicion.*

*As far as MORRIS is concerned everybody is guilty until proved guilty which is undoubtedly what they are. ALICE spots him and panics, rummaging under one of the seats to pull out a rolled up length of red carpet. MORRIS lets a few people notice him then gives a sharp blast on his whistle. This shocks the whole tram to attention.*

MORRIS: *[through gritted teeth]* Kindly have your tickets ready for inspection thank you, ladies and gentlemen!

MORRIS *opens his coat slightly to flash an inspector's badge at them. Then, tipping his hat to her.*

MORRIS: Miss Katranski, very good evening to you.

ALICE: *[deferential]* Hullo, Mr. Stanley, very good evening to you, sir.

*She bows and unrolls the red carpet in front of him as she backs down the centre aisle. He takes the carpet literally in his stride.*

MORRIS: *[producing an official notebook]* So how's it going tonight?

ALICE: *[almost too quickly]* Fine!

MORRIS: Just fine?

ALICE: Very well, thank you, Mr. Stanley.

MORRIS: No special problems?

ALICE: None at all, sir.

*When the red carpet runs out he holds a shoe up, she goes down on her knees to begin spit and polishing it.*

MORRIS: *[checking off the list in his notebook]* No drunken disorderlies?

ALICE: No.

MORRIS: Hooliganism?

ALICE: No.

MORRIS: Vandalism? Graffiti?

ALICE: No.

MORRIS: Fare refusals?

ALICE: Nup.

MORRIS: Noise problems, smoking?

ALICE: Nup.

MORRIS: Complaints from passengers?

ALICE: *[looking round at them hopefully]* Not that I'm aware of. *[She finishes one shoe, he lifts the other.]*

MORRIS: Pregnant women rushed to hospital?

ALICE: No, but there was a discovery of parenthood late in life.

MORRIS: *[looking at her dubiously]* Well, I don't quite understand that but I suppose it's a tick.

ALICE: Thank you sir.

MORRIS: *[returning to the list]* Loud yelling, screams of any sort?

ALICE: Heaven forbid.

MORRIS: It does happen you know.

ALICE: No unusual noises.

MORRIS: Refusals to leave the tram on issuance of an order directly from yourself?

ALICE: I don't think so...

MORRIS: Think so?!

ALICE: No, no, nothing like that at all.

MORRIS: Pretentious conversations, people showing off?

ALICE: Is that against the rules?

MORRIS: I find it offensive.

ALICE: True.

MORRIS: Driver's performance?

ALICE: *[thinks about it]* 8 out of 10.

MORRIS: *[accusingly, checking his watch]* He's two minutes late!

ALICE: The lights across Dandenong Road were very slow tonight.

MORRIS: It better not happen again. *[Snapping away his notebook]* So, nothing in particular to mention? No untoward behaviour?

ALICE: It's been one of the most pleasurable trips I've ever had the privilege to enjoy, Mr. Stanley.

MORRIS: Good, excellent, we at the Met like to see a contented workforce. It is, I believe, the fundamental underpinning of any real increase in productivity. *[He pulls his shoe away from her cleaning and turns to the rest of the tram.]* So. How's she been going, eh? Looking after you all, has she? *[Bending an ear to the passengers]* I'm *sorry* I can't hear that.

ALL: *[egged on by* TERRY] Yair-s.

MORRIS: Good, well, now for the most important part. *[Spelling it out]* Has - she - sold - you - all - a - ticket!?

*He pulls a huge magnifying glass from inside his coat pocket, polishes it with a hankie and stabs a look of intense suspicion at the culprits that lie before him.*

MORRIS: Right! Tickets thank you ladies and gentlemen!

*And he goes about microscopically inspecting every aspect of their travel cards]*

MORRIS: Thank you...thank you...*[handing them back]* thank you...

ALICE *blanches as she remembers* TERRY *not buying a ticket, shakes a fist at him behind* MORRIS's *back.*

*She tries to give him one but can't quite manage it without* MORRIS *seeing and anyway* TERRY *just laughs at her predicament.*

*Occasionally* MORRIS *pauses over one and gives that person a savage look.*

MORRIS: What's this rubbish? *[Finding some tiny fault with the ticket]* You call this a valid ticket?

MORRIS: It's got more scratches than a green tree monkey. How many months ago did you first start using it? Rubbish! *[Tearing it in half and flicking the pieces in the air behind him]* Don't leave the tram, until I've come back to fine you.

*SAM realises that at last there is someone in authority who she can complain to.*

SAM: Excuse me, inspector.

MORRIS: Thank you...thank *you...[concentrating on other passengers]*

SAM: Inspector...

MORRIS: Just a minute madam.

SAM: But inspector.

MORRIS: Will you wait your turn please! *[Behind his back* ALICE *is trying to restrain* SAM.]

SAM: *[to* ALICE] But I have to tell him.

ALICE: *[whispering]* Please, you'll cost me my job!

SAM: *[ploughing on]* You shouldn't have to put up with it.

*Meanwhile* MORRIS *has worked his way towards* TERRY *who has slipped on a pair of sunglasses and stands holding the dog.*

*At first* MORRIS *reacts as the magnifying glass wanders over the strange outline of the dog, he leaps back with a shock, then taking in the whole picture* MORRIS *beams at* TERRY, *all sympathy and concern.*

MORRIS: *[to* TERRY] Ah, well done, lad. Good to see you out there, in the community, trying. It's the kind of plucky spirit that made this country what it is today. Now we at the Met have had our fair share of trouble from disabled people protesting at all the closures, the lack of wheelchair access, the conversion to light rail and so on...and I'm here to say that you're a shining example that not all the physically challenged brigade are a pack of ratbags...

*He takes some coins from Alice's bag and pops them in the slot cut into the dog's head, patting the dog.*

MORRIS: Look after him now, boy, you're all he's got.

SAM: *[unable to contain herself, breaking away from* ALICE'S *muffled protests]* Inspector!

MORRIS: *[suppressed anger]* I said I'll be with you in a minute madam!!

SAM: *[standing her ground]* I'm sorry but there's a youth on this tram...

MORRIS: Will you shut-up MADAM! *[Turning back to inspect more tickets]*

SAM: *[running straight on]* He stole that dog, accosted me personally. and just a moment ago threw an old man out the doorway!

MORRIS: Who him? *[Pointing at the passenger whose ticket he's currently checking]*

SAM: No HIM! *[Indicating* TERRY]

MORRIS: Don't be ridiculous, woman, this fine young cannibal's disabled. *[Stops, baulks.]* My god, what did I say?

ALICE: Cannibal?

ALICE slumps into a seat realizing the game is up. This mad woman is going to cost her her job.

MORRIS: *[rounding on* SAM] You see, you've got me doing it. It's exactly the sort of mealy-mouthed small-town prejudice gallant people like him have to put up with from smarmy know-alls like you all the time. You ought to be ashamed of yourself.

SAM: *[Whipping the sunglasses off* TERRY, *who stares blindly ahead, blinking vacantly]* He did not buy a ticket and he is not blind.

*Morris takes his own glasses off to get a better look at* TERRY *and obviously begins to have doubts. He looks down, pinches the bridge of his nose, looks around at the tram and takes a deep breath.*

SAM: Go on you silly little man, ask him for his ticket.

ALICE: *[blustering in]* He just got on, I haven't reached him yet.

MORRIS: *[holding up his hand for silence, then gently to TERRY]* Could I trouble you for your travel card, sir?

TERRY: *[fanning out a dozen or so used travel cards, some playing cards, footy swap cards]* Certainly, pick a card, any card.

MORRIS *reels back in shock, throws his glasses back on - only to discover that they are* TERRY'S *sunglasses, he shoves them back at* TERRY *and puts his own glasses on - taking a look at several of* TERRY'S *"tickets" in turn.]*

MORRIS: February 31st? Scratch and Match? Instant Tatts? *[Ripping them to shreds]* Rubbish. Rubbish. Hoh, rot! Absolute bunkum. Miss Katranski. *[Clicks his fingers]*

ALICE: Oh, please, Mr. Stanley, please don't...I've got a mother, sir, she, she's an invalid pensioner and we couldn't manage without (my salary)...

MORRIS: Pull yourself together, woman!

ALICE: *[snaps to attention]* Sir!

MORRIS: Sell this...this creature a ticket and then hand in your badge.

ALICE: Oh, please sir, no...

MORRIS: You can consider yourself stood down as of *[checking his watch]* 12.43 pm *[stops]* that's not right *[puts his watch to one ear, shakes it, looks around meekly]* Has anybody got the time?

ALICE: *[ripping her badge off, flinging it down at his feet]* You bastard!

MORRIS: Look on the bright side it saves us having to retrench you and get into trouble with the unions. Yes, I love 'natural attrition.' Even the word itself has a certain gutsy ring to it. Tell Tran Van Tong to shunt at the top of Swanston Street then take this tram straight back to the depot.

ALICE: Why should Tran listen to you. You'll be sacking him next.

MORRIS: That's right, Miss Katranski. You've hit the nail right on the pantograph. Driverless trams! We already have them on the drawing board. The entire Melbourne system will soon be run by a computer barely larger than your earrings. And frankly I can hardly wait for that day. I'll take your money pouch. You can send in the uniform by parcel post.

ALICE: They'll retrench you too you know. Inspectors will become redundant like the rest of us.

MORRIS: *[self-confident smile]* I hardly think so.

ALICE: Oh no?

MORRIS: No, you see because we're all going to become tour guides! *[He triumphantly unfurls a small Japanese flag on stick and holding it above his head, blows his whistle then picks up a megaphone testing it.]* Osaka, Nagasaki, Kyoto...

TERRY: *[to* ALICE*]* Great, this means you can come out with me.

ALICE: I never want to *see* you again.

MORRIS: *[through the megaphone - all smarmy and ingratiating again]* Ladies and Gentlemen, permit me to expose myself to you for a moment... *[raising his hat to them]* Morris Stanley, Assistant Inspector of Timetables at the Melbourne Metropolitan Tramways Department and part-time architectural historian. As you know the Met has been running a special Commuter Bonus Package all week that includes a free walking tour of old Melbourne with every travel card purchased. This evening's tour will include such historical marvels as the Flinders Street Railway Station, St. Paul's Cathedral and Young and Jackson's Hotel where we will shortly be stopping for a refreshing and authentic taste of some genuine Australian malted ales...*[He takes out a Japanese Phrase Book and delivers the following in a kind of halting, pidgin-Japanese]* Young and Jackson's hotel was founded by Norman Young and Henry Jackson who made a killing in New Zealand mining ventures. The hotel was built on land granted to John Batman founder of Melbourne for which he paid 100 pounds. The present building was originally erected as a hay and corn store and later became Miss Cook's school for young ladies...

*However he's interrupted by* SAM *who has been looking anxiously across at the Arts Centre in St. Kilda Road.*

SAM: Oh - they've all gone in!

MORRIS: *[perplexed]* What?

SAM: Stop! Stop the tram!

ALICE *pulls the cord for her.*

MORRIS: What's going on? *[Pained]* Oh - you're leaving are you?!

SAM: If this is an example of what public transport is all about then it's an absolute disgrace. It's the most upsetting journey I've ever been on.

MORRIS: And where is madam going, may one ask?

SAM: *[proudly]* The Australian Opera.

MORRIS: *[contemptuously]* The Australian Opera! So - my little tour's not good enough for you, eh?

SAM: I couldn't think of a greater waste of time in the entire universe. You pathetic cockroach.

*[The tram stops and she sails off, hurrying across the road to the opera theatre at the Arts Centre.]*

MORRIS: *[yelling back at her]* Oh yes, go on then, go off to your boring proscenium arch musical. All those tedious fat bitches with horns on their heads screeching as if a brick's stuck up their arse! See if I care. You're bypassed lady. Don't you realise what a brave experiment my *Melbourne By Torchlight Excursions* really are? Why bother coming on a tram if you don't stay for the entertainment? What's the matter with the Rolls tonight? Air conditioning not working? Hairdryer run out of batteries? If you'd brought a broom you could have flown there! You're bypassed lady, bypassed! I hope you drop your jaffas!

*Head held high* SAM *continues on into the Arts Centre pointedly ignoring him. Back on the tram* MORRIS *clutches his heart and mops his sweating brow, breathing hard, almost exhausted from his manic reaction to* SAM'S *exit.*

MORRIS: *[quieter, hoarse now]* Excuse me if I seem a little distant from time to time, ladies and gentlemen. It's just that I have a slight flutter of the heart and a tendency to perspire a lot. *[Spitting it out]* Australian Opera! Has anyone got any valium? Bex? Any powders? No? No... I guess not. *[Bitter again]* There's always someone who *walks* isn't there? Always somebody who leaves. I'll take Panadene ... No? OK *[picking up megaphone and Japanese flag again]* Anybody else want to leave? No. Just as well. Right. Now when we get off I want you to stick near the flag and where possible hold hands. We don't want to get mixed up with the other rabble do we? And please, try to pretend you're not all from St. Kilda. This is a fairly fashionable hotel. Right, now where was I before I was so rudely interrupted...*[checking the phrase book, and again in halting Japanese]*...school for young ladies. Its most famous item is the painting of Chloe by Jules Lefebvre which was brought to Melbourne for the Great Exhibition in 1880. The real Chloe is said to have taken her own life. Norman Young purchased the painting for 800 guineas in 1908.

*The tram finally pulls in to the stop on the corner of Swanston and Flinders Streets.*

MORRIS: Ah yes, here we are. *[Japanese]* As we alight from the tram you will notice on your left the very famous Flinders Street Railway Station. *[Lifting the flag high]* Now follow me everyone, stick together, and please wait for the traffic lights, we lost three pensioners last week...

*And so the audience follows* MORRIS *to Young and Jackson's for interval refreshments. The tram moves on to shunt at the top of Swanston Street with a rather despondent* ALICE *still being hassled by* TERRY.

# INTERVAL

Morris Stanley (Roger Selleck) and some audience members from the 1991 production of Storming St. Kilda enjoying interval together at the famous 'Chole's Bar' in Young and Jackson's Hotel.

*Half an hour later the tram returns to the stop opposite Young and Jackson's and the passengers, still lead by* MORRIS *and his Japanese flag, all get back on. He's been giving them a rave about the history of St. Paul's Cathedral situated behind the stop. And invites them to participate in a souvenir photograph of their enjoyment of one of his Melbourne By Torchlight Excursions:*

## ACT TWO
## Outward Journey

*However when* MORRIS *finally manages to herd them onto the tram he soon becomes aware that* ALICE *is still there, still cleaning and still being hassled by* TERRY.

TERRY: Look, I just want to apologise, you know - 'bout your job and everything.

ALICE: I told you, I never want to see you again.

MORRIS: Miss Katranski -

TERRY: Well, let me make it up to you by taking you to a disco or something.

ALICE: Go away!

MORRIS: Miss Katranski what are you still doing here?

TERRY: Butt out, pal, this is between her and me.

MORRIS *is just a teeny bit intimidated by* TERRY.

MORRIS: Excuse me, but Miss Katranski has just been sacked.

TERRY: Good, then you can't give her any more orders. *[Back to* ALICE] Come on just one dance.

ALICE: I'm sorry, I'm tired and depressed I just want to go home to bed.

TERRY: *[putting an arm around her]* OK!

ALICE: *[shrugging him off]* By myself!

*She disengages from him and turns back to cleaning the windows, one last polish before she goes.*

TERRY: Well, how about a game of space invaders?

ALICE: Are you deaf or something? I said I'm tired.

TERRY: Just one game.

MORRIS: Miss Katranski -

TERRY: *[brushing MORRIS aside and focusing squarely on ALICE]* That what you want to do all your life? Clean windows, work as some wage slave, get hassled by ratbags?

ALICE: I'm being hassled now.

MORRIS: *[taking her bottle of window spray]* Miss Katranski, there's no need to do anymore work on this tram.

ALICE: I can't go 'til it's spotless. Don't you understand? It was my tram. I'm responsible for it until it gets to the depot... *[almost breaking down]* for the last time.

MORRIS: Oh - very well. *[He hands her back the spray bottle]*

TERRY: What about tomorrow night?

ALICE: I'll be looking for a new job tomorrow.

MORRIS: At last it sinks in.

TERRY: The weekend?

ALICE: I'm an emergency blood donor, I'll be on standby.

TERRY: You mean stand*off* don't you.

MORRIS: *[impressed]* I didn't know that. Jolly good show, Miss Katranski. With that kind of spirit I'm sure you'll obtain another job. We're always looking for toilet cleaners at head office.

ALICE: *[angry]* I don't want to be a cleaner. I want to be a connie. I may seem like just another ordinary dumb worker to you but this job meant more to me than anything else in the world! I'm a tram fanatic. A gunzel. Do you know what that means?

TERRY: No.

ALICE: It means I dream about them at night.

TERRY: Geeze.

ALICE: I go tram spotting on the weekends.

TERRY: Can I come too?

ALICE: I had an electric tram set even before I could walk. I *love* trams.

TERRY: I won't let it affect our relationship.

*But* ALICE *ignores him, almost in a trance now.*

ALICE: I love the sound they make when they squeal around corners. I love the bell the driver dings when some mug motorist is blocking the tracks. I love their shape. I love their colour. I love their woody interiors and the sparks that fly when the pole comes off. And one day, one day ... there won't be any other form of transport.

*Incredibly* TERRY *produces a ukulele and strums out a musical beat to* ALICE'S *rave.*

ALICE: No cars [cord]

ALICE: No buses [cord]

ALICE: No planes [cord]

ALICE: No trains [cord]

ALICE: No trucks [cord]

ALICE: No bikes [cord]

ALICE: Just - cargo trams, dining trams, very, very, very fast trams. Trams to Sydney [cord]
And trams to Perth [cord]...

*Accompanied by* TERRY *on the guitar* ALICE *bursts into song.*

ALICE: When... the...dri-ver.
When the driver smiles at me I go to Richmond...
Or to Balwyn
Got my bag on
My suit and smile on
Got both shoes on,
Then we drive on...
Now, I have a responsibility
That makes me feel humility
And integrity...
At which point I should mention the power
of my Tra-vel Ca-rd!!

TERRY: *[joining the chorus]* Oh ho ho!

MORRIS, *who has been happily tapping away to the music now puts his whistle to his mouth and blows it in time.*
*Like a deeply unbalanced Latin dancer he joins in a mad tango with* ALICE *up and down the centre aisle. It's a weird Hollywood musical moment.*

ALICE: When the inspector-
When the inspector climbs aboard
My legs start shakin'
And a quakin'
When they pile on
I put my smile on
And off we go again ...
Turn around again [ALICE *and* MORRIS *turn.*]
And then back again *[they bump backsides]*
Wo - wo, oh - oh!
When the driver -
When the driver smiles at me
I go to Richmond.

TERRY: Or to Balwyn.

ALICE: Or to Burwood.

TERRY: Or to Hawthorn.

ALICE: Or East Brunswick.

TERRY: Or to Broady.

ALICE: Hartwell!

TERRY: Spotswood!

ALICE: Geelong! Hong Kong!

MORRIS: *[suddenly breaking off the dance]* Trams don't go to Geelong, Miss Katranski. *[The music stops.]*

ALICE: Not yet they don't.

MORRIS: Oh I see, well, one can't help but admire your optimism.

TERRY: Does that mean she gets her job back?

MORRIS: No. I'm afraid not, my decision is final.

MORRIS *takes out a detective comic and soon falls asleep behind it. The tram stops half way down St. Kilda road and a fairly inebriated* SAMANTHA *staggers back on.*

SAM: Oh, hullo Miss Katranski, darling, the same tram! What a nice surprise. You know I've walked all this way down St. Kilda Road and I still couldn't catch a cab.

TERRY: They won't stop for drunks, love.

ALICE: Terry!

SAM: Well I have a right to be drunk. You know why? You know what tonight is? Tonight is the last night of my short and *Les Miserablés* life.

ALICE: Oh no. You mustn't say that.

SAM: It's alright dear, there's nothing left to live for.

ALICE: Don't be silly, you're young, rich, you're enormously privileged. Incredibly lucky. Reasonably good-looking.

SAM: *[laughs humourlessly]* Rich! Privileged!

ALICE: Didn't you find Michael?

SAM: Yes, unfortunately.

ALICE: What did he say? How was he?

SAM: Wet, when I left him.

ALICE: Oh.

SAM: Yes, when he finally emerged at interval and broke the news I tipped a champagne cocktail all over his Stafford Ellinson with the cutaway pockets.

And you know my dear it was such a liberating experience I ordered another one and did it again.

Then I decided to get seriously phissed. Now I'm going home to take all my clothes off and leap naked into the swimming pool and I simply don't care who sees me.

TERRY: Mind if I come?

ALICE: *[elbowing* TERRY *aside]* What was the news? What did he say?

SAM: He's lost it all the bugger. That skunk, that pile of dead tissue I married ten years ago has just informed me that our entire fortune, the Paris flat, the Brighton mansion, the cars, the mink I keep in Geneva, the yacht in Ibitha *[starting to slur her words]* - it's gone, the lot of it. It was like he couldn't wait to tell me. I think he even *enjoyed* telling me.

ALICE: Gone? Where?

SAM: Prudential Mortgage Trustees. Ever heard of them?

ALICE: No.

SAM: You will. It'll be front page in all the gutter press tomorrow. Michael was a director. It appears there's a teeny weeny little shortfall in the books. The auditors have just rejected Michael's Profit and Loss statement. The only good thing about it is - he'll probably go to gaol.

ALICE: Yeah, prison can have a bad effect on people. *[thinking of her mum]*

SAM: I hope they throw the key away. *[Rummaging in her bag for a cigarette]* You know what this means?

TERRY: Ah let me guess - you won't be able to afford a new frock for Cup Day.

SAM: Worse than that! I'm going to have to find a job!

ALICE: You're not the only one.

SAM: I said to him, I said 'What am I supposed to do?' He said 'You're going to have to earn a living like everybody else.'

ALICE: I'll be down the dole office myself tomorrow. *[Gently takes the cigarette off her]* Sorry.

SAM: Oh yes *[puts her lighter away]* I forgot. No smoking. I'm always forgetting. *[Bursts into tears]*

ALICE: *[putting an arm around her]* It's alright.

SAM: *[through tears]* As if I haven't already worked my fingers to the bone for that incompetent blob. I decorated the house. I personally ordered all the paintings. I co-ordinated the landscaping, drew up the dinner lists, I even bought his stupid clothes. He was wearing *flanellette* shirts when I first met him.

ALICE: How awful.

SAM: Yes. Why I ever saddled myself with such a scurnbag is beyond me. Do you know what the Australian Opera will symbolise for me from now on?

ALICE: No.

SAM: The end. The end of ten years of being buried in Brighton. I mean, if I don't make a stand now I'll never be free of him. He was just so passionless. We only did it once a week, Sunday morning.

ALICE: I suppose that's better than the national average.

SAM: Yes, well it *was* about as exciting as going to church.

TERRY: Hey, lady, I wouldn't complain if I lived in Brighton with a swimming pool.

SAM: Oh, but you've got so much spark about you blackhead.
You and Miss Katranski, both.

ALICE: Alice. Just call me Alice, love.

SAM: Alice, yes, thank you, that's very kind of you. Look, *[bright idea]* why don't we have a little party back at my place. A few drinkies and a nude swim?

TERRY: *[putting an arm around her]* Sorry, lady, but Alice is coming to my party.

SAM: Oh, yes, of course, Brighton is the pits isn't it. No one with any spark would want to go there. It's just that you see tonight's... tonight's...my birthday *[breaking down, a flood of tears.]*

ALICE: *[sympathetic]* Aw -

SAM: I thought - that's what I thought we were doing tonight, I thought he was taking me to the opera to celebrate. But he didn't even mention it. He...he'd completely forgotten. *[More tears]*.

TERRY *picks up his ukulele again and starts strumming the tune to 'Happy Birthday'. All the passengers join in. Overcome* SAM *cries through the whole song,*

*The tram stops again and* NIGEL *and* CATHY *come back on. His hair is wet from a bath and he carries a towel around his shoulders on which is sewn the word 'Tickles'.*

NIGEL: *[Still rabbiting on, oblivious to the fact that it's the same tram and people are still listening]* I mean, god! We live in a world where you can watch several movies every night - just on television. I really wonder what effect that has on us. In the old days people saw a movie maybe once a week. There was time to think about it and discriminate. Now it's just like a blur. Scripted drama is all around us. We're totally *moved* out. I just don't think people can tell the difference between fiction and reality any more.

CATHY: Well you obviously can't.

NIGEL: What do you mean?

CATHY: You'd rather make a film than have a kid, wouldn't you?

CATHY *starts coming on to* NIGEL. *Almost teasing him with faux affection.*

NIGEL: Sure I wanted to have kids, Cathy, but I wanted to have them in a stable situation you know?

CATHY: *[suddenly pulling back, the romantic moment over]* Stable? We lived in a stable remember? Out the back of Johnno's place.

TERRY *spots an opportunity for some fun and wanders up to* NIGEL

TERRY: Hey I really like the way your girlfriend moves. Mind if I sing her a song?

NIGEL: *[scarcely believing it]* What?

TERRY: She a bit of a goer, then?

CATHY: What am I a lamp-post? You can ask me if you've got any questions?

TERRY: *[smiling at her]* I like it when you're sultry.

CATHY: Jesus!

TERRY: Get's me all hot.

CATHY: Are you for real?

TERRY: Touch me, I'm real.

CATHY: Thanks, but I don't want to catch anything.

TERRY: Funny, too.

NIGEL: Look mate...

TERRY: I like a girl with a sense of humour.

CATHY: Why don't you just hop on your skateboard and
go home to mummy.

TERRY: Makes you really attractive.

CATHY *groans.*

NIGEL: Look, mate, you know, I wouldn't flirt with her if
I was you. I just don't think she's interested.

TERRY: *[slipping his hand around NIGEL's throat]* That's
alright, cause I'm interested in you too.

NIGEL: *[spreading his arms wide, backing off]* Look we've only got a few minutes, alright, and we'd just like to have a quiet chat, OK?

TERRY: Mind if I listen in?

CATHY: Yes, so just piss off.

NIGEL: Hah!

*NIGEL leaps back and adopts a threatening Kung Fu stance
pumping the palms of his hands at TERRY.*

NIGEL: Hah! Hah! HAH!

*Rather than be intimidated though,* TERRY *comes casually forward, grabs one of* NIGEL's *palms and simply twists his fingers right back.* NIGEL *groans and drops to his knees, in pain and humiliated.*

TERRY: I'm only trying to be friendly.

CATHY: Forgodsake, just GO AWAY!

TERRY *lets* NIGEL'S *hand go, leaving him on the floor trying to work the blood back into his fingers.*

TERRY: OK, OK, no hassles, right?

NIGEL: *[from the floor]* Sheeah! This is so Melbourne.

TERRY: *[back to CATHY]* I just felt really attracted to you, that's all. How many people feel really attracted and never say it? There's too much holding back. We're always holding back on what we really feel.

CATHY: I think I could contain myself.

TERRY: *[holding out his hand for CATHY to shake]* 'Long as there's no hard feelings.

CATHY *folds her arms, turning away refusing to have anything more to do with him.*

NIGEL: Cathy -

CATHY: What?

NIGEL: He's going.

TERRY: *[still holding out his hand]* Yeah, I'm going.

CATHY: I can hardly wait.

TERRY: Shake.

NIGEL: He won't go otherwise.

TERRY: I won't go otherwise.

NIGEL: *[almost pleading]* Cathy -

CATHY: Look, you shake his bloody hand, you're so fond
of him.

*She collects her bag and moves up the other end of the tram.* TERRY *turns to* NIGEL *who's dusting off his knees as he stands up.*

*TERRY:* Shake.

NIGEL: *[hesitates, then tentatively takes* TERRY'S *hand]* Shake.

TERRY: *[pumping* NIGEL's *hand longer than* NIGEL *feels
comfortable* with] They say you can tell a man's personality by his handshake. Not much to you is there, Tiger?

TERRY *lets go and* NIGEL *shakes his hand to get the blood pumping again. He comes back up to* CATHY.

CATHY: You really showed him, Nigel.

NIGEL: Don't worry, Cathy, he won't bother us again.

CATHY: Especially with you around to protect us.

NIGEL: Anyway, I'm not sure this is such a good idea.

CATHY: What?

NIGEL: Going back to meet your mother.

CATHY: It's only for a cup of tea.

NIGEL: I'm not sure I'm ready for her yet. I mean I'm poised at a crucial turning point in my life path. I may need guidance.

CATHY: She's mellowed, alright?

NIGEL: So she's just an ordinary, run-of-the-mill harpy now?

CATHY: Ever since she moved down here she's been on a learning curve. I think it's tremendous for a woman of her age.

NIGEL: Learning curve, huh? Well, that's good because she
never read my poetry.

CATHY: Nigel, *millions* of people never read your poetry.

NIGEL: I'd like to read something now, if I may. *[Unfolding a scrap of paper.]*

CATHY: Please, Nigel, it's been a long day.

NIGEL: It's kind of weird really, almost psychopathic, cause I was thinking about kids just the other day, the idea of having kids and the kind of world they're growing up in now, and I found this poem, Cathy, my first important sonnet. I'm dedicating it to Dennis ..

CATHY: Darryl.

NIGEL: Right, yes, Dedicated to Darryl by Nigel Davidson, B.A...
*[adopts an oratorical pose then:]*
Oh Muckdonald's why am I always looking at your children's playgrounds through barbed wire...'

TERRY *has started a free-form musical accompaniment to the poem on his ukulele. It's about as dreadful as the poem.* NIGEL *breaks off reading.*

NIGEL: Do you mind, excuse me.., this is a work of art.

TERRY: A wank of what?

NIGEL: You wouldn't have the foggiest idea of what it takes to be an artist, would you? *[To the rest of the tram]* Does anybody here have any idea of the sort of commitment that involves?

SAM: I did macrame once. Does that count?

NIGEL: Only if it's about the poetry in one's soul. Great art is all about great feelings.

TERRY: Yeah we know what you feel. Eventually it'll send ya blind.

NIGEL: *[boring in on* TERRY*]* I mean what happens to YOU when you look up at the stars at night? Huh? Are they just dots in the sky? Or does some overwhelming primal fear take over - of just how small and insignificant we really are? In the whole vastness of the universe we're just a brief candle burning brightly for a fragment of cosmic time. One flash and we're gone. *[Again to the rest of the tram]* I mean, look up at the stars, just crane your heads out through the window and take a good hard look up there.

TERRY: *[looking out]* It's cloudy.

NIGEL: What?

TERRY: It's cloudy, you can't see any stars.

NIGEL: Oh, of course. This is Melbourne isn't it? You poor saps just don't get a chance, do you? No wonder you all think you're so significant down here.

*The tram stops near where* DANNY *got thrown off so unceremoniously on the way in. Terry has started strumming his ukulele again, serenading* ALICE *who is fairly unimpressed. However, it means* TERRY *has his back to the door when an enraged* DANNY *roars back on brandishing a rolled up 'Truth' newspaper.*

DANNY: *[Whacking* TERRY *about the head with the paper]* Hey! Remember me? Eh? Son? Smartarse. Very funny eh? Think it was hilarious did ya?

*Pandemonium breaks out, people are screaming.* NIGEL *is taking photos and recording it all on his Sony Walkman. This is a potential story.*

TERRY *puts up a feeble defence against the thrashing newspaper, trying to protect his head, backing up*

*one end of the tram, lifting a leg to shove* DANNY *away from him.* DANNY *manages to grab* TERRY'S *raised foot and drag him back towards the door.*

DANNY: You're getting off.

TERRY: *[Hopping on one leg]* Hey, watch the instrument, mate. *[Hands his ukulele to a passenger for safekeeping.]*

DANNY: See how you like it.

TERRY: Hey, no, listen, it wasn't me mate, it was the driver. I thought he would've waited for ya. The way he just took off like that, I tried to tell him. I said 'Hang on mate, the old codger wants to get back on.'

DANNY: Bullshit. You're off pal, you're going for a walk.

TERRY: Give me me foot back.

DANNY: Off!

DANNY *tries to shove* TERRY *through the open doorway. This is serious, so* TERRY *easily wrenches free of* DANNY *and twists his arm up behind his back shoving him back up the tram.*

TERRY: Settle down, you old coot, you'll blow a gasket.

DANNY: Bloody young punk bastard I'll kill you! *[still trying to whack TERRY backwards with the rolled up newspaper]*

ALICE: Terry! Stop it!

*She tries to separate them while SAM comes up to MORRIS who, incredibly enough, is snoring on through it all behind his crime comic.*

SAM: Inspector! Mr Stanley, there's an atrocity being committed.

MORRIS: *[sleepily]* Wha ...?

SAM: Do something!

*And then it hits him - literally, TERRY sends DANNY barrelling into MORRIS, knocking them both over and ultimately sending DANNY and MORRIS sprawling onto the floor on top of each other.*

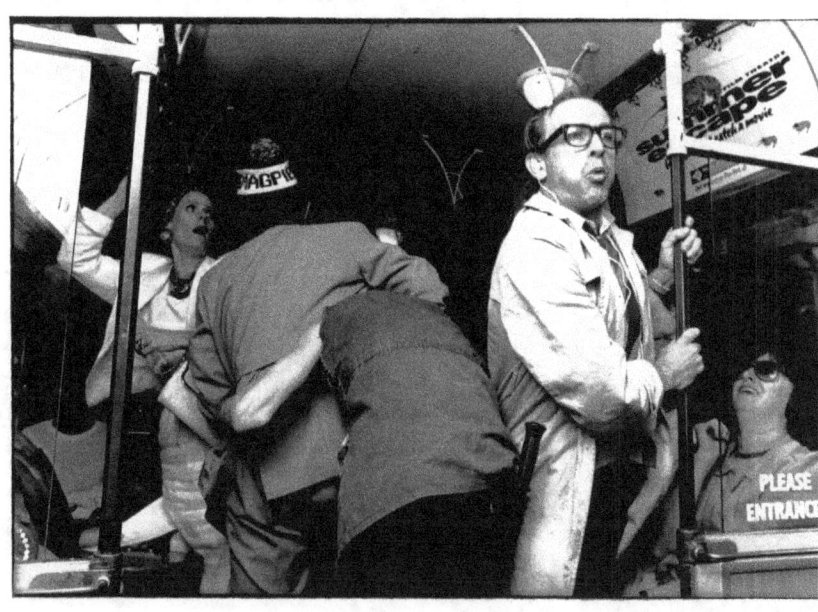

TERRY: *[laughs]* There's no need to hug him! Watch out mate he'll be kissing you next.

SAM: *[to Morris]* Are you in charge here or what?

DANNY: *[struggling to his feet]* I'll bloody kill you!

TERRY: You've flipped your lid you stupid old derro.

DANNY: STUPID!

TERRY: OK, OK, you're not stupid, you're a genius fercrissake! I thought the exercise would do you good.

DANNY: I'll give you exercise you germ!

*And with a superhuman effort DANNY slams TERRY into the rear driver's door. There's a sickening thud. MORRIS is nervously blowing into his whistle but in his breathless agitation no sound comes out.*

TERRY: Right, that does it!

*Holding his head, TERRY produces a knife. There's a shocked pause.*

DANNY: Now listen, mate...

TERRY: *[suddenly really vicious]* No, you listen for a change you mangey old derro.

*With a sudden mad fire in his eyes TERRY advances on DANNY who stumbles back, really terrified now. Finally MORRIS'S whistle works! He gives a shrill blast on it and bravely comes past DANNY to confront TERRY head on.*

MORRIS: I am an official representative of the Melbourne Metroplitan Transport Authority and I'm ordering you to sheath that knife at once.

TERRY: Ordering me to what? *[lurching up to him, twisting the knife manically under MORRIS'S chin. SAM screams.]*

ALICE: Terry!

MORRIS: *[taking an uncertain step back]* Alright, alright...I'm strenuously urging you to p...p...

TERRY: *[again the wild dancing eyes]* To WHAT!?

MORRIS: To, to p p p put the ... I'm warmly encouraging you t t t to...

TERRY: *[eyes on fire]* ENCOURAGING!!??

MORRIS: Suggesting. I'm just it's just a suggestion that's all, don't take it too seriously.

TERRY: SERIOUSLY!!?? *[knife held in front of him,* TERRY *continues to advance menacingly on the rapidly disintegrating* MORRIS, *the passengers' protector]*

MORRIS: Alright, alright, I'm pleading OK? *[shaking at the knees, putting up his notebook and magnifying glass as a pathetic shield, not taking his eyes off the knife for a moment.]*

MORRIS: Pleading, begging, I'm I'm *reasonably* firm about it.

TERRY: Get down on your knees and bark like a dog.

MORRIS: *[Can't believe it]* Wha...? Now listen...

TERRY: Go on, bark! dog!

MORRIS: Dogs are *not* allowed on trams!

TERRY: *[lashing out with the knife in all directions]* You wanna to get cut!?

MORRIS: *[immediately drops to his knees and starts barking]* Woof! Woof! Woof!

TERRY: Good, now we understand each other - man to dog.

MORRIS: Of course, sir, I'm trying to see it entirely from your point of view.

TERRY: Bark when you talk to me, Dog!

MORRIS: Woof, woof, woof.

ALICE: Terry! You'll get us all arrested, Is that what you want?

DANNY: Ah what do punks care about the working class, love. You'd have to be in a liquid metal band before he'd listen to ya.

SAM: Isn't it marvelous that people can air their differences like this in public.

MORRIS: *[still on his knees, thrusting his badge forward]* You see that badge, you know what that badge means?

TERRY: Bark!

MORRIS: Woof! Woof, woof.

DANNY: The bands you listen to nowadays have got about as much musical talent as toilet flushing.

TERRY: *[aiming the knife at him]* Sit on that and swivel, commo.

MORRIS: *[appealing to DANNY]* P-p-please don't antagonise him.

TERRY & DANNY: *[together]* SHUT-UP!

ALICE: Put it down Terry.

TERRY: *[ back to DANNY]* So you reckon you know about punks do ya mate? Then you know why I dress like this?

DANNY: There's nothing to know, you're as vacant as a parking lot.

TERRY: I dress like this cause I'm living in poverty.

SAM: I thought you lived in Malvern, that's where you got on.

TERRY: I'm an aussie child, see, and it's 1991, so how come I'm still living in poverty? Is that right, is that fair? Cause if I'm still poor like this I reckon some dickhead's stuffed it up.

DANNY: Christ, he's a frigging political genius.

SAM: I thought he looked like a young Liberal.

NIGEL: Hang on, hang on. He was about to tell us why he dressed like this. Irrespective of where he comes from or what party he votes for, it's obviously important to him. I suggest he dresses like that because, well for the same reason *[to* SAM] you dress like that or *[to* MORRIS*]* Why he wears this ridiculous Sherlock Holmes costume.

MORRIS: I BEG your pardon!?

NIGEL: *[leaning down to* MORRIS] Because he wants to be noticed.

TERRY: That's right, 'cause when I walk down the street see, and some dickhead stares at me, I says 'What are you lookin' at turd features'.

DANNY: Brilliant! absolutely brilliant. Sheer poetry.

MORRIS: Now listen, just put the weapon down before you cut yourself. My grandmother got a stiff thumb from a knife like that.

TERRY: You know I think I'll slice your head off right now.

ALICE: Shut-up! Everybody just shut-up! This is my tram and I'm in charge! *[Supportive cheers all round]*

MORRIS: You're a good lad and you've got a bright future
ahead of you.

TERRY, ALICE, DANNY, NIGEL: *[all together]* SHUT-UP!

MORRIS *retreats on all fours, barking. cringing under a seat next to some poor passenger's legs.*

ALICE: *[to TERRY]* Now stop being so bloody stupid and put the knife away.

TERRY: Will you come out with me?

ALICE: *[to MORRIS]* You see, you see why we're needed?
*[to the PASSENGERS]* This is exactly the sort of incident that gives public transport a bad name.

TERRY: I'll put it away if you say 'yes'.

ALICE: You want to drive people off their own form of transport? Is that what you want? Force everybody to buy a car?

DANNY: You're talkin' to a brick wall love, you'd have
to be on Playschool before he could understand ya.

ALICE: *[coming forward, holding out her hand]*
Give it to me.

TERRY: They'll throw the book at me!

MORRIS: I give you my solemn word as senior public servant there will be no further action taken.

ALICE: You hear that? Now give it to me.

TERRY: Say you'll come out with me.

ALICE: Maybe...

TERRY: Not good enough *[menacing the knife back at MORRIS]* Bark!

MORRIS: Woof, woof, woof. Forgodsake Miss Katranski say 'yes'.

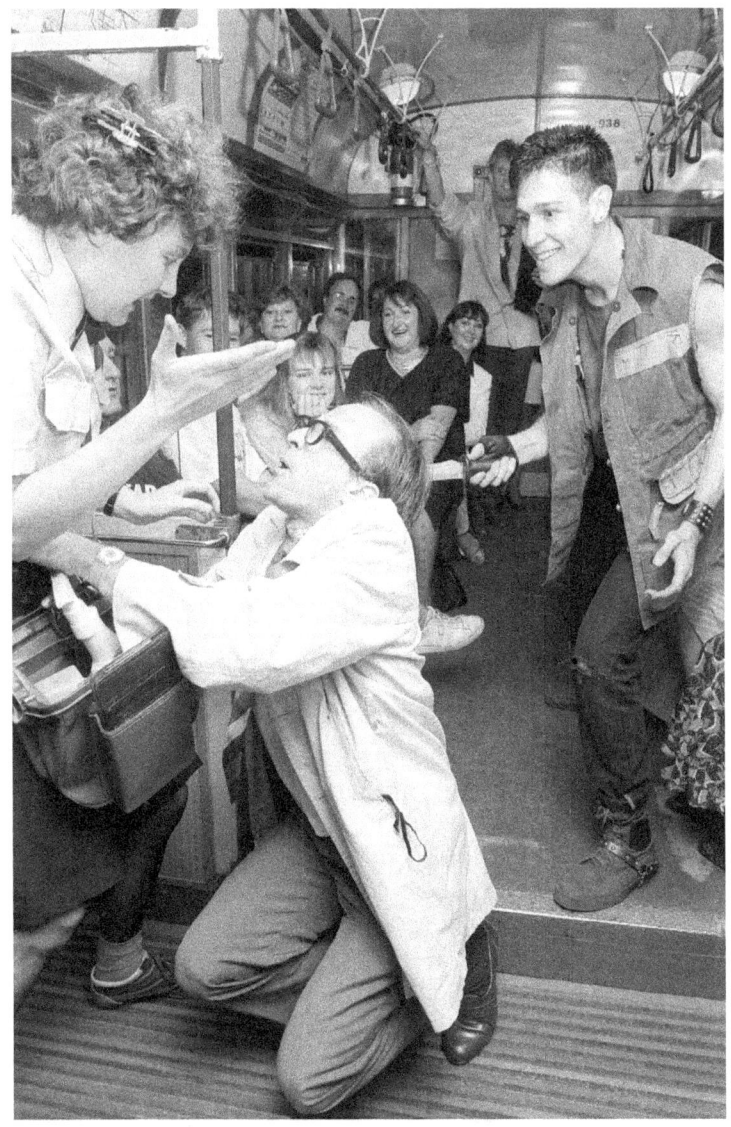

ALICE: Will you give me my job back?

MORRIS: Anything, anything.

ALICE: Promise?

MORRIS: I'll personally sign a letter to the Chief Superintendant of Timetables.

ALICE: *[back to* TERRY*]* Alright, dammit, yes, I'll go out with you. Now give me the knife.

TERRY *grins, savouring the moment, turns the knife handle safely towards* ALICE *and slowly hands it back to her. The tension evaporates.*

SAM: *[applauding]* Well done, Alice, bravo.

MORRIS: *[brushes the dirt off his knees, and stands up]* Yes, fine effort, Miss Katranski, I'll take matters in hand now thank you.

*As soon as he takes the knife off her* MORRIS'S *face immediately contorts with pent-up rage. He slams* TERRY *back against the driver's door and holds the knife to his throat].*

MORRIS: Right you bloated filth. My daughter's in traction because of a vegetable like you, and the only thing stopping me from ramming this knife into your fetid guts right now is the delicious thought of you making car number plates for the rest of your unnatural life!

ALICE: But you gave him your word.

MORRIS: I wouldn't give him the carrots out of my vomit if he was starving in the gutter! *[Making a big lunge at* TERRY *with the knife]* You ANEURISM!

SAM *screams,* TERRY *rears back and* ALICE *intercepts* MORRIS's *lunge just in time. She deftly slips the knife out of his hand.*

MORRIS: But M - Miss Katranski

ALICE: You said you wouldn't.

TERRY *slips in between them and easily retrieves the knife from* ALICE.

TERRY: Thank you Miss Katranski. *[tables turned again,* TERRY *pushes* MORRIS *back against the door and raises the knife to lunge at him.* MORRIS *gasps in horror.]*

DANNY *comes up behind* TERRY]

DANNY: Thank you Mickey. *[He slips the knife out of* TERRY'S *hand and grabs* MORRIS *in a headlock with the knife next to his ear]*

MORRIS: Hey, listen, mate - no, look!

DANNY: *[pulling* MORRIS *towards the rear of the tram in a half nelson]*
Get back! Get back!

MORRIS: Get back! Get back!

DANNY: I'll kill him!

MORRIS: He'll kill me! Could someone call a doctor? I suffer from a serious heart condition.

DANNY: Don't move! Don't move!

MORRIS: Don't move! Don't move! Miss Katranski, help!

DANNY: Right! Now. I'M HI-JACKING THIS TRAM!

*Most people laugh at the absurdity of it. But* SAM *faints while* NIGEL *gets his camera and starts taking shots again.*

TERRY: Ah Bullshit.

MORRIS: Please don't antagonise him. I could die! Look
*[pulls out a wallet of photographs]* Look, you see my wife, my family, my Rottweiler, they depend on me. *[His wife is dressed in uniform, possibly that of a prison warden.]*

DANNY: Disgusting, put it away.

MORRIS: Yes, of course, sir, I'm completely at your disposal.

DANNY: Are you just, well that's real good, 'cause I got on this tram early this afternoon, well before the second race, with the simple intention of going straight home. For eight hours I've been trying to get there and now I'm mad as hell and I'm not gunna take it anymore.

MORRIS: Fair enough, that's perfectly understandable.

DANNY: Oh you think so, do you? Well that makes a very nice change because what I want you and Miss Katranski here to do is really very, very simple.

MORRIS: Oh good, excellent, I think I can speak for both of us.

DANNY: I just want you to turn this bloody tram around and take me straight back to St. Kilda.

TERRY: Ya mad, ya stupid old coot.

DANNY: Oh, am I just, mad, eh? And what are you, you - you're a mob of gutless wonders. Not one of you could give a tinker's curse about the plight of a poor old digger, wounded for his country, chucked off a tram by some young Nazi. Nobody lifted a bloody finger. When this sort of thing happens in broad daylight can the gas chambers be far behind? You're the me me me generation, couldn't give a stuff about anything.

SAM: Oh, that's not true surely.

DANNY: The only good thing you can do with Brighton love is put a *bomb* under it. Yuppies here, yuppies there, yuppies all over the place. Hanging out in their bloody cappuccino bars with their sunglasses on and their poofy hairdos. The only good thing you can do with a yuppie these days is shoot the bastard and put it out of its misery. I'm so mad now I just want to Kill Kooyong, Trash Toorak, Slaughter South Yarra, by christ! I'm going to retake St. Kilda *BY STORM*!

ALICE: Well, you'll need a travel card!

DANNY: I just about paid with me life for this ride, mate.

MORRIS: *[feeling the knife tighten round his throat]* Miss Katranski!

ALICE: Anyway, we can't turn round.

DANNY: Yes, you can!

MORRIS: Miss Katranski turn this tram around and take this good gentleman back to St. Kilda.

ALICE: I can't do it.

MORRIS: Yes you can.

ALICE: No I can't.

DANNY: I want to go back.

MORRIS: He wants to go back.

ALICE: You can't go back. This is a tram, it doesn't go backwards.

DANNY: But I want to go back.

MORRIS: He wants to go back.

ALICE: But we can't go back.

DANNY & MORRIS: WHY NOT!?

ALICE: Because we're already *GOING* to St. Kilda!

MORRIS *sinks a little at the knees which only brings his chin perilously closer to* DANNY'S *knife.*

DANNY: Now don't try and confuse me, miss, just turn the bloody tram around, cause we're not stopping until I see Luna Park.

ALICE: Alright I'll go and get Tran to shunt the bloody tram at the next shunt point and take you straight *BACK TO THE CITY!*

DANNY: *[perplexed]* Well how come I was facing backwards when we were going the other way? *[still obviously totally confused about directions]*

ALICE: *[pointing]* Have a look at the destination roller.

DANNY: Where?

MORRIS: *[pointing behind them]* There!

DANNY *swings unsteadily around,* MORRIS *seizes the opportunity and reaches for the knife.*

DANNY: Hey! Hey!

*They struggle clumsily over it, with* MORRIS *banging* DANNY's *hand back against the strap rail, and then* DANNY *wrenching his hand down between them. Each is as hopeless as the other at fighting and despite the grunting and groaning little real damage is done.*

*However, while the knife is down between their legs* DANNY'S *grip slips and it accidently plunges up into his mid-section. His back arches up away from the knife and he collapses in a heap on the floor with* MORRIS *overbalancing on top of him. There's a sickening groan from* DANNY *and his body goes limp as Morris flops down on top of him.*

TERRY: Hey now, cut that out fellas. No humping allowed on trams. No bromances thank you very much.

*But* MORRIS *is aghast as he slowly drops the knife and stares at his hands. They're covered in a gooey red mess.*

*He seems to be in a trance as he steps back unable to believe it. Blood!. He displays his red smeared hands to the passengers and like an automaton reaches for the cord to stop the tram.* DANNY *remains slumped in a lifeless, silent heap on the floor.*

MORRIS: *[smiling weirdly around at the passengers, obviously quite demented now]* I wonder if I remembered to take the chops out of the freezer. I like a nice cut of lamb after work. And I'll have to get a pint of milk on the way home. Thelma hasn't had her shots this week, either, have to remind her about that. [A *sudden mad yell]* They never told me the job'd be like this! *[Starts ripping up his detective comic]* Rubbish. Rubbish. Hoh! Rot! Bunkum. That travel card's way out of date *[on his knees appealing directly to a passenger]* I didn't mean to do it! Woof woof. You saw him. He... he pushed me. He... *[laughs]* I'm cracking up *[laughs, tries to vomit, can't, laughs]* Cracking up!

NIGEL: *[coming forward with a card]* Listen I can give you the name of a really good stress management consultant. Try her, you won't regret it.

MORRIS: *[still in a trance]* This tram's late. Take it straight back to the depot. You heard me. You're all sacked. *[Laughs]* Report to my office immediately.

*The tram stops and he backs off down the steps, wide eyed with fear, showing his hands to motorists stopped beside the tram before staggering off into the night.*

MORRIS *[To various motorists and pedestrians wandering past]* You saw it. He pushed me. I ... I didn't mean to do it. Get this car back to the depot immediately. You're sacked. We have robots to replace you.

*The tram moves on and as he disappears behind them* ALICE *throws back a hopeless appeal*

ALICE: Morris, Mr. Stanley, come back!

SAM: He'd make a wonderful Macbeth.

NIGEL: He reminds me of her *mother. [Indicating* CATHY]

CATHY: Stop exaggerating.

NIGEL: *[to the same passenger* MORRIS *appealed to]* Why didn't you do something? He'll probably tear the head off a cat now.

CATHY: Nigel, shut-up!

ALICE: Look what he's done to my nice clean tram! *[Dissolving into tears on some passenger's lap. Meanwhile* DANNY *is up on all fours, groaning and crawling around.]*

DANNY: He's bloody killed me the bugger.

SAM: Perhaps I can help, I've done a course in bandaging and animal husbandry at the Elwood leisure centre.

DANNY: *[climbing unsteadily to his feet, and grabbing the knife from where* MORRIS *dropped it]* And it's all his bloody fault!

*He lunges at Terry with the knife, the women and* NIGEL *scream.* DANNY *stabs - and* TERRY *merely holds up his palm. The knife thuds in but bounces straight back out.* DANNY *stabs in again but again,* TERRY *easily deflects the blow.* DANNY *halts. Then tries the knife on his own palm. Same thing. It goes in and bounces straight back.*

DANNY: What? It's a bloody trick knife! A plastic bloody trick knife!

*The relief is obvious, suddenly both* TERRY *and* DANNY *are laughing. Then* DANNY *remembers the red goo oozing out of his stomach. He sniffs his fingers and opens his shirt to reveal a mangled pie and tomato sauce.*

DANNY: Me lunch! *[pulling out the bits of pie]* The bastard's stabbed me lunch! *[Holding the mess up]* Who's going to pay for this then? I thought I was dead, ya bastard. I could see the headlines clearly: 'Inspector knifes pensioner between residences.' Not the sort of poetry I had in mind for my final demise.

TERRY: Ah look, you've got tomato sauce all over me knife. *[Wiping it clean on* DANNY'S *coat.]*

DANNY: *[pulling his coat away]* Get out of it!

ALICE: *[to* TERRY] I'll never forgive you for this.

TERRY: What did *I* do?

NIGEL: What did anybody do? Nothing. Not a thing. Nobody does, nobody cares. I plunge the knife into his brain and nothing happens.

NIGEL *does so and the knife bounces in and out*

NIGEL: No brain. Nobody home.

*Then it all suddenly hits* NIGEL. *He's rubbing his temples.*

NIGEL: I mean what am *I* doing? This isn't reality. This is a nightmare. Here I am on a number 69 tram going back to her mother's place. I've got to get off, I've got to get out of here. *[Goes to a door, but of course it won't open between stops.]*

*DANNY:* I think he's got a touch of cabin fever.

CATHY: She'll grow on you, alright?

NIGEL: She grows on me like a rare skin disease. Every time I see her I smell napalm.

CATHY: Do you want to see Darryl or not?

NIGEL: Yes! *[hesitates]* No! *[more pacing up and down]* I ... I don't know. She hates me.

CATHY: She's mellowed, alright!

NIGEL: She has a voodoo doll of me and I know she sticks pins in it. I know she'd like to kill me. I know I'd like to kill her.

CATHY: Your imagination is bad for you.

NIGEL: Oh, so being an artist isn't good enough for you huh.

CATHY: That's right, that's why I want Darryl to be an accountant. I want his life to amount to something.

NIGEL: Guilt was always your art form, Cathy.

CATHY: Nigel, I'm not dragging you home, this was your idea remember?

NIGEL: *[making another move for the door]* It's all this tension, my biorhythms are out again. I'm not sure if I can face her.

CATHY: Well, *go* then, see if I care.

NIGEL *stands there nodding for a moment. Really pissed off now.*

NIGEL: Alright then, fine.

CATHY: Look, I'll even pull the cord for you.

NIGEL: Don't do me any favours, Cathy.

CATHY: No, you're doing *me* a favour. Get off.

NIGEL: OK, OK I'm going.

CATHY: Good.

NIGEL: *[surprised by the ease with which she can say it]* Yeah?

CATHY: Good, good-bye.

NIGEL: I'll probably never see you again.

CATHY: That'll be a relief.

NIGEL: I said, 'ever again.'

CATHY: That's what you promised last time. I didn't
believe it then, either.

*The tram stops again and the doors slide open. About to step off,* NIGEL *hesitates, comes back up to her.*

NIGEL: Why isn't this traumatic for you?

CATHY: You're boring.

NIGEL: *[that really hurts]* What? [CATHY *stifles a yawn.]* I'm ...?

CATHY: You're boring - go away.

NIGEL *just hangs there for a moment, holding his briefcase. He just can't believe it.*

NIGEL: I'm not boring. I don't *bore* anybody.

CATHY: How do you know?

NIGEL: I've asked people.

CATHY: I rest my case.

NIGEL: Christ, Cathy, you're the mother of my only child, we're practically related.

CATHY: And never got a cent for it.

DANNY: Give it to him, love.

NIGEL: *[hurt]* It was really good to see you, you know that? Half an hour ago I was really happy.

CATHY: I'll be happy when you're gone.

NIGEL: Why can't you see how attracted I am to you?

CATHY: Yes, I've finally realised there is a film script in you Nigel, because you're a *walking tragedy*!

*The tram remains stationary, doors still open. Everyone waiting.*

NIGEL: *[finally angry, backing off the tram, down the steps onto the roadway]* Well stuff it, Cathy!

CATHY: And stuff you *[moving away again, finally]*.

*NIGEL nods again, looks down and then makes a determined exit off the tram. Acting as dramatically as he can.*

NIGEL: *[from the roadway]* And stuff Melbourne and stuff
your mother! I gave you the best years of my life! Nothing but blood, sweat and tears!

*NIGEL swings round to storm off into the night, straight into the arms of an on-boarding policeman:* **SNR CONSTABLE WARREN WILKINSON.**

WARREN *pushes* NIGEL *ahead of him back into the tram.*

WARREN: Just step back inside, son.

NIGEL: What?

CYRIL: *[Coming up behind Warren]* Step back inside please.

NIGEL: What is this?

**SNR CONST. WARREN WILKINSON and CONST. CYRIL FOSTER** *block the open door, ending any hope of* **NIGEL** *escaping.* **CYRIL** *pulls the cord to start the tram and it moves on again.*

WARREN: We've just had a report about 'blood' on this tram.

NIGEL: Blood!?

CYRIL: Yellow cab, five minutes ago radio'd D24 with a clear description of grievous bodily harm.

NIGEL: I might have yelled a little we didn't get to the bodily part.

WARREN: Don't be crude, son.

SAM: *[coming forward]* But, officer, it wasn't a real murder it was only his lunch that got stabbed.

WARREN: Whose lunch got murdered?

ALICE: The old man who bought it thought he was dead, but it was only his pie and sauce.

DANNY: Come to arrest a meat pie have ya?

CYRIL: What was only a pie and sauce?

ALICE: His lunch of course.

WARREN *and* CYRIL *share a knowing look.*

WARREN: Fruitcakes, Cyril.

CYRIL: And not even a full moon, Senior.

SAM: But Mr. Stanly, the inspector, he's gone off in a terrible funk thinking he was responsible.

WARREN: Responsible for what?

ALICE: The murder.

WARREN: *[taking out a notebook]* Were threats of violence uttered?

NIGEL: Christ, mate, I only said I'd *like* to kill her - I didn't really mean it.

WARREN: Kill who?

NIGEL: *[indicating* CATHY] Her mother! She'd like to kill me.

WARREN: And where's the said woman, now, son?

DANNY: And where's your helicopter? Makes more noise than a sick chook in a cyclone. What is it this week, Operation Himmler? Dob in a Derro?

WARREN *and* CYRIL *turn from* NIGEL *and move menacingly towards* DANNY *who staggers back to the rear of the tram, throwing his arms up in the air.*

DANNY: Hands up, hands up, you're all under arrest.

WARREN: *[nods towards* NIGEL*]* Cuffs on that one thank you, constable.

CYRIL: Right you are Senior.

NIGEL: *[As* CYRIL *snaps the cuffs on him]* Ah what? What is this? *[looking over to her, pleading]* Cathy ...?

WARREN: Stick him on the hand rail for the time being. Looks like we'll just have to take them one at a time.

NIGEL: *[as he gets cuffed to the rail]* Look, I'm Nigel Davidson, you know? The film-maker? Some of my work's been on Channel Seven - you must've heard of me.

WARREN: *[impressed]* Channel Seven?

NIGEL: Yes, I do free ads for blue light discos. I've even directed an episode of *Crime Stoppers*. You must've seen the one about the Balwyn snow dropper? They caught him with an armful of underwear in K Mart.

WARREN: Really?

NIGEL: And this is the thanks I get?

WARREN: *[tentative]* Do you... do you ever audition people?

NIGEL: I'm casting for a Toyota musical right now. We're launching the new Land Cruiser.

[WARREN *immediately breaks into an audition song, accompanied by* TERRY *on the guitar. At the end* WARREN *turns to him, arms wide, breathless, hopeful.*]

WARREN: Well, what do you reckon?

NIGEL: *[looking him up and down, unimpressed]* We'll let you know.

WARREN is *incredibly hurt by that.*

WARREN: Oh, I see. 'Let me know,' Have me hang by a phone for the next three months going quietly mad whenever it rings and it's not you.

NIGEL: Look, it's nothing against you personally, it's just that I've got some people from *Cats* coming.

WARREN: So an ordinary copper's not good enough for you, eh?

NIGEL: I didn't say that.

WARREN: That's just the kind of mealy mouthed prejudice we've come to expect against the working class. It makes my blood boil!

DANNY: Watch out, he's going to arrest the lot of us! Hands up, hands up, you're all under arrest.

*DANNY raises his hands which causes the sleeves of his old coat to fall down revealing about half a dozen watches strapped to each arm.*

WARREN: Ah ha! Grab those arms, deputy constable.

CYRIL *[squirming]* Oh - do I have to ?

WARREN: Police work's a hands on job I'm afraid. *[Stabbing the words back at* NIGEL*]* We can't all be show ponies or prima donnas.

*Keeping as far away as he can,* CYRIL *takes one of* DANNY'S *arms and holds it gingerly by a couple of fingers.*

WARREN: *[to* DANNY*]* Now son, would you mind telling me how you allegedly came into possession of the said watches - I asked at ... *[looks to* CYRIL*]* at...? at...?

CYRIL: *[checking a passenger's watch]* Oh, at 10.08, Senior.

WARREN: Procedure, constable. Come on son, the evidence, keep your wits about you.

CYRIL: Oh, sorry, constable, I asked at *[reading the watches on* DANNY'S *arm]* ah, at 10.09, 10.11, 10.20, 12.18, 7.45 am, and Mickey's big hand is missing on the last one.

DANNY: Look - me brother-in law's a jeweler in Richmond, fercrissake.

WARREN: Not a very good one either, pal, selling watches that slow, it's almost criminal.

CYRIL: I'm taking these arms to be used in evidence against you.

WARREN: *[to* DANNY*]* And you can drop the blasphemy, son, unless you wanted it added to the list of charges.

DANNY: What list of charges?

WARREN: Receiving, disturbing the peace, exposing yourself - you're under arrest pal.

DANNY: You can't do this to me I'm a full member of the Collingwood Football Club.

WARREN: *[waving his breath away]* Well, you're *full* alright, whether you re-member is another matter entirely.

WARREN *and* CYRIL *think that's hugely funny.*

WARREN: Cuff him to the handrail Cyril.

*As* CYRIL *does so,* SAM *has had enough champagne cocktails to throw herself into the mix just for the hell of it. Perhaps she sniffs a hint of scandal for Michael.*

SAM: And I'm one too. Officer, I'm terribly, frightfully, awfully guilty. I poured two champagne cocktails all over my husband's receding hairline and then I went and stole a glass from a leading Melbourne theatre company. I demand to be taken into custody.

WARREN: *[Still preoccupied with* DANNY*]* Yes, yes, all in good time madam...Now what's this about a stabbing?

WARREN turns *back to face* DANNY

DANNY: It's not my fault, it's all because of that punk rat hiding down the back. He stole a blind dog and wouldn't give me me money back. He was the one who brought the knife. Geeze, I never wanted to come on this damn fool trip anyway. I just wanted to go home to St. Kilda.

CYRIL: You're not going anywhere, pal, till we've bashed a statement out of you.

WARREN: *[warning]* CYRIL !

CYRIL: *[recalling correct procedure]* Oh, ah, until you have volunteered to help us with our investigations by ah...

WARREN: *[prompting]* Making a ...

CYRIL: Making a statement.

WARREN *breathes a sigh of relief.*

DANNY: Look, I've made enough bloody statements tonight to last a lifetime. I told these people before I've called it quits politically. When I said 'bomb Brighton' I didn't mean *bomb* in the technical sense .

WARREN & CYRIL: *[reeling back]* BOMB!

DANNY: It was more a figure of speech you know, alliteration, like 'Bugger Beaumaris' or 'Bury that Briefcase'...

WARREN & CYRIL: *[still both reeling]* BRIEFCASE!

WARREN *swings round and freezes on seeing* NIGEL *cuffed up the front and clutching his briefcase to his chest.*

WARREN: Clear the forward saloon!

WARREN *quickly retreats to the extreme other end of the tram*

WARREN: Well go on, Deputy Constable...

CYRIL: What?

WARREN: Clear the forward saloon, bomb disposal procedure pages 8 to 11 -*[throwing him an instruction manual for bomb disposal]*

CYRIL: Oh - do you think I've got the experience?

WARREN: I know you can do it. Page 8, now come on lad, hop to it.

CYRIL: But Warren...

WARREN: Quickly, Cyril. Procedure, son. You could get us both a Governor's medal for this.

CYRIL: Why do I always have to do the bombs?

WARREN: You see those stripes. *[Indicating his superior rank]*

CYRIL: *[reluctantly]* Oh, alright, *[quoting the manual]* 'Pull over driver ... Oh sorry *[flipping to another page]* - ah yes, here we are ...

WARREN: Come on son, quickly, it could go off at any second.

CYRIL: *[quoting from the manual as he moves tentatively towards* NIGEL] Now everybody just stay calm and remain perfectly still, this is an extreme emergency and your lives are all in considerable danger. But please do not panic as the slightest motion could trigger a massive explosion and that would be really yukkie. *[frowns back at* WARREN] Are you sure this is right, Senior?

WARREN: Absolutely, well done Deputy Constable. Just stay there for a sec.

*Everyone is reeling back from NIGEL further isolating him and making it difficult for him to dispose of his briefcase out through a window.*

WARREN: *[To Nigel, nervous]* N-n-now son, I just want you to stand perfectly still, breathe as gently as you can - I'll mention this co-operation to the magistrate - and tell me quite frankly: what is in the briefcase?

NIGEL: Oh shit!

[NIGEL *has been holding his briefcase defensively close to him. But in his nervousness he accidentally flips the catch and the lid flies open. A film can, small camera, some girlie magazines, a toothbrush, a teddy bear, a shirt, tie and some undies tumble out onto the floor.*

WARREN *hits the deck, diving behind a couple of passengers.* SAM *closes her eyes and puts two fingers in her ears.*

NIGEL: Officer, you've got the wrong man!

WARREN: We'll decide who the wrong man is you clumsy idiot! Now what's in the Teddy Bear and be quick about it.

NIGEL: How dare you!

WARREN: Alright then, what's in the film can?

NIGEL: That's undeveloped and, irreplaceable documentary footage.

WARREN: Open it up Cyril and watch out for tremblers.

DANNY: Watch out for knee tremblers, Cyril. *[laughs]*

NIGEL: I'm warning you, if you open that can you'll destroy the only record in the entire world of Prince Charles and Lady Di riding the Big Walrus at Sea World.

CYRIL: That could be important, Senior.

WARREN: Are you questioning my authority?

CYRIL: No, but...

WARREN: If it looks like exploding just throw yourself on top of it and try to save the rest of us.

ALICE: Well, I'm not going to clean that mess up.

CYRIL: Couldn't we just ring the army?

WARREN: You want them to get all the credit?

CYRIL: No, but they are the bomb experts.

WARREN: Look, with all this wanking going on it could explode at any moment. Open it Constable, come on, son.

*Gingerly* CYRIL *opens the lid of the film can to reveal a plastic bag full of green herbal material. He smiles and relaxes immediately.*

CYRIL: I don't think it's a bomb, Senior.

WARREN: *[laughs, coming forward to take the bag of dope]* I think you're done son. You're well and truly cooked, Mr. Big Time Musical Director.

CYRIL: I don't think it's a film either, Senior.

WARREN: *[holding it up]* Oh yes it is, it's `How Green Was My Valley'. *[Laughs, CYRIL laughs with him.]*

CYRIL: Or `Green Acres'. *[They both laugh, slapping their knees with glee. WARREN is relaxed now, confident, back in control.]*

WARREN: 'Green Mutant Ninja Turtles'.

NIGEL: Look, I made a mistake, okay - that's the tin with my Colt's Foot tea in it.

WARREN: Doesn't look like any part of the horse that I recognise.

DANNY: That's wacky tabacy.

NIGEL: I go to a naturopath, it cleanses the bladder. Cathy - will you tell him about my circulation problems.

WARREN: Don't reckon you'll have any circulation problems for the next five years or so, pal. Stash like that. You're gone son, you're down for a dealer.

NIGEL: Will you stop trying to sound like someone out of `The Bill.' Cathy - will you tell him: it's *Colts Foot tea* forcrissake! It's a simple, natural, medicinal herb.

CYRIL: We have another name for it son: 'cannibal's saliva' *[laughs - again echoed by WARREN]*

NIGEL: Cathy, will you tell them about my special bladder complaint?

WARREN *follows* NIGEL's *look, realises who he's addressing and comes up to* CATHY, *notebook ready.*

WARREN: Are you apprised of the defendant's identity, miss?

NIGEL: Look, officer I already told you, I'm Nigel Davidson, see *[offering his card]* Nigel Davidson Productions?

WARREN: *[ignoring him]* Well, miss?

*All eyes are on* CATHY, *there's a tense pause while she thinks about it, takes a deep breath, then...*

CATHY: I've never seen him before in my life.

WARREN: *[putting away HIS notebook, pulls the cord to stop the tram]* Thank you.

NIGEL: Ah what!

WARREN: Come on Nige - let's see how well you sing down at the station. We've got one cell with a really lovely echo. *[To* CYRIL*]* Uncuff the other villain, Constable, and attach him to Mrs. Champagne Cocktail. I'll take our film director personally myself.

NIGEL: *[to* CATHY*]* Thanks for nothing. I mean you're not interested in any part of my body are you!

WARREN *starts leading* NIGEL *off the tram as* CYRIL *pushes* DANNY *and* SAM *(who are cuffed together) ahead of him. As the mad scrum goes past* TERRY *he manages to lift the bag of dope out of* WARREN's *back pocket. Putting a finger to his lips. Urging the passengers to stay 'mum'.*

SAM: *[to another passenger, handing them Nigel's camera]* Would you mind taking a photo? This is my first arrest.

*While* SAM *poses proudly with* DANNY. *The dialogue as they go off occurs simultaneously:*

NIGEL: You could have told them, Cathy, you could've told them about my bladder.

SAM: *[stepping off the tram with* DANNY *in tow]* Could somebody call my husband, M. Hart-Byrne, Church Street Brighton? Tell him his wife will be talking to the press down at the St. Kilda police station.

WARREN: Yeah, tell him we're all down there having a nice cup of Colts Foot tea. *[CYRIL and* WARREN *laugh]*

NIGEL: *[still to* CATHY, *resisting, being pulled away by* WARREN*]* Well, what about a kiss? Not even a kiss good-bye? At least Judas gave that much.

DANNY: *[As* SAM *drags him off]* This is a bloody outrage I tell ya I've never seen this young mug in me life *[indicating* NIGEL*]*. What's it got to do with me? I like to have a lot of watches. Is that a crime to tell the time now?

NIGEL: Cathy, Cathy, call a lawyer, call amnesty, I did a free ad for them on Channel Four. I'm dying out here, man. This is political! I'm bleeding to death, Cathy. My bladder!

SAM: And don't forget to all come back to my place so we can take our clothes off and go for a rudey nudey dip...

*All bunched in together,* POLICE *and* ARRESTEES *constitute a mad scrum of writhing bodies out on the footpath.* NIGEL *tugs on* WARREN *like some big kid being dragged away against his will. He props up against lamp-posts, fire hydrants, wrapping his legs around them, anything to hold himself back from being dragged off.*

*As the tram moves on they gradually disappear from sight. And for a few moments, peace, in the form of silence at least seems to settle on the tram as people resume their seats after straining for a view of the mad fracas outside.*

*Then suddenly,* ALICE *lashes out at the person she knows to be the real culprit.*

ALICE: *[pummeling* TERRY*]* Why didn't you say something?!

TERRY: *[pulling back]* What?

ALICE: Why didn't you tell them what happened?

TERRY: How do you expect anyone to have respect for trams if that's the way people carry on!

ALICE: You're incredible.

TERRY: You know why there's graffiti all over the place? Cause no one cares about the trams and trains. No one cares about nothing. Why should kids care?

ALICE: None of this would've happened without that stupid knife of yours.

TERRY: It was only a toy forcrissake!

ALICE: And look at all the trouble it caused.

TERRY: Well, at least the old coot's got a bed for the night. It's better than his usual rubbish bin.

ALICE: Two people are in gaol because of you.

TERRY: Hang on, I'm not responsible for her nerdy boyfriend.

CATHY: He's not my boyfriend!

TERRY: You could've stuck up for him or somethin'.

CATHY: For five years I stuck up for him, with him, at him. Picking up the mess he left behind, solving his problems. And for what?

TERRY: He *will* be up for dealing with a stash like that.

CATHY: Ah come off it.

TERRY: Eight years I tell ya, that's what the law says.

CATHY: He won't get eight years.

TERRY: He'll get a few. *[Turns to a PASSENGER]* Isn't that right? *[The PASSENGER nods]* See, he's been in prison.

CATHY *takes a deep breath.*

TERRY: Eight years sharing a cell with some filthy murderer or sexual pervert.

CATHY: It'll do him the world of good. He'll just make a film about it when he gets out.

TERRY: If he hasn't turned into a hardened criminal by then. *[indicating the previous* PASSENGER] Like this bloke here.

CATHY *seems uneasy, she's clearly wavering.*

CATHY: Look, you know what I do for a living? Do you think I want to get hassled by the cops?

TERRY: They'll break him in there. Darryl's dad will come out a ruined man.

CATHY: He's ruined already. *[She takes another deep breath, pinches her nose, looks down at NIGEL'S briefcase and its contents strewn over the floor. She bends down and finds a scrap of paper.]*

*I* mean - *[holding up the poem]* look at this: *[reads]*

'Oh MuckDonald's, why am I always
Looking at your children's playgrounds
Through barbed wire?
Sealed off there, McDonald Duck
Mc Reagan, Mc Napalm, Mc Donald
Ronald, corporate death burger.
*[she breaks off reading]*
He's obsessed, he's obsessed with Donald Duck and Ronald Reagan!
*[reads on]*:
'You evil clown, Ronald, you shark,
Who do you think you are kidding, frozen hamburger?'
*[looking round]* I'm supposed to save this?
*[back to the poem]*
The same old neon restaurant,
Same old yellow sign,
Cloned a thousand times,
Through the brick mushroom suburbs
Of the mind...'

*She folds the paper thoughtfully then appeals around to the tram generally*

CATHY: Really, am I supposed to go back to the cops and plead for this sort of thing to be let loose upon the world?!!!

ALICE: *[trying to be positive]* It does have a certain ring
to it.

TERRY: Oh yeah, it's real good, love, they'll soon bash that sort of stuff out of him in J division.

CATHY: *[reads the last bit at the bottom]* Dedicated to Cathy Waterman who gave me the best years of my life, Nigel Davidson B.A. November 11th 1985. *[Folds the poem away.]*

ALICE: *[changing her mind]* Yeah, no. He needs help alright.

CATHY *squats down and gathers together the scattered debris of* NIGEL'S *briefcase.*

CATHY: *[pulling the cord]* Alright, alright. I'll bail him out, but he's going to be on the first plane back to Sydney tomorrow morning. And he's sleeping in the spare room.

*The tram stops and* CATHY *gets off. Alice looks anxiously out the doorway after her.*

TERRY: Is she going? Is she doing it?

ALICE: Yeah.

TERRY *and* ALICE *jump for joy, embracing and laughing at their success.*

TERRY & ALICE: Great, we did it, ha, ha, it worked!

*Then* ALICE *disengages, suddenly coming to her senses.*

ALICE: Why do you have to look like that?

TERRY: Like what?

ALICE: Like some hopeless case with nowhere to go.

TERRY: That's the way I am.

ALICE: Well I don't like it.

TERRY: What's wrong with it?

ALICE: I don't want to go out with someone who looks like a reject from a ska tissue band.

TERRY: What's wrong with ska tissue?

ALICE: It's too loud, it's too boring and ... it's not ... *[softens]* what you really are, Terry.

TERRY: How would you know?

ALICE: Because I know that deep down underneath that ... that grubby exterior there's a really nice, decent young man.

TERRY: Ah, yuk!

ALICE: It's only a costume, Terry. *[spots NIGEL'S shirt and tie left behind on the floor]* Look, try these on...

TERRY: You gotta be joking!

ALICE: Go on, just for me.

TERRY: I'd rather spew.

ALICE: Do you want to go out with me?

TERRY: *[hesitates, then indicates the PASSENGERS]* Make them close their eyes.

ALICE: Just try it on, that's all I'm asking.

TERRY: Only if they don't watch.

ALICE: OK everybody, close your eyes.

*And so, reluctantly, TERRY puts the shirt on.*

ALICE: And the tie... *[holding it out]*

TERRY: *[spotting a passenger]* She's peeking!

ALICE: Come, it won't kill you. *[Gets the tie on him]* There, see, that's not so painful is it? *[Looking for a PASSENGER the same size]* Now what about a nice pair of trousers? *[The PASSENGER she's glancing at looks petrified]* Alright a coat then. *[Borrows a coat from another passenger and when she's got the coat on* TERRY *she displays him to the rest of the tram]* OK open your eyes everybody.

TERRY: Hang on!

ALICE: There see, doesn't he look nice?

*The* PASSENGERS *overwhelmingly agree.*

ALL: Yairs...

TERRY: Here, give us a look in the mirror. *[Turns to check his reflection in the glass door]* Ah yuk I look like a bank clerk.

ALICE: No - you look like a... a nice young doctor.

TERRY: A doctor? *[Turns to another* PASSENGER] Hey, lady I'm a doctor, can I do an internal? *[Laughs]*

ALICE: Sing us something, Terry, sing us something...nice.
[TERRY *retrieves his ukulele from the passenger who was minding it for him and sings a beautiful love song to* ALICE.]

At the end of which it's clear that she's fallen for the rogue.

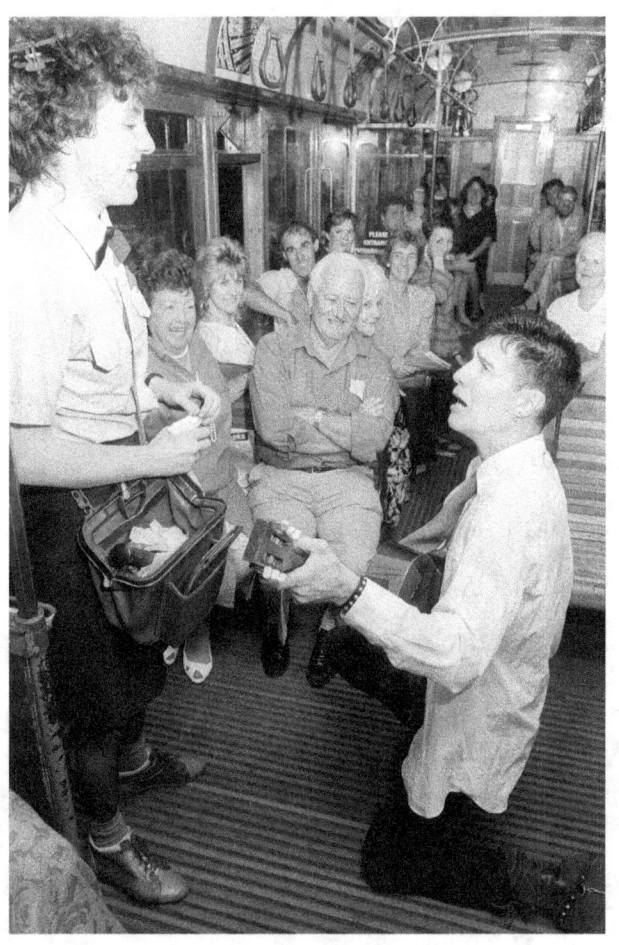

ALICE: *[dreamily]* See, you could be anything you want. I bet you could walk into the Melbourne Club right now and nobody would even notice.

*That rings alarm bells!*

TERRY: What! Nobody? *[He quickly rips off the shirt, coat and tie and gives them back to her. By now the tram has returned to the St. Kilda Beach terminus from which it started.]* I'm going to MacDonald's over there for three minutes. Just enough time for two Big Macs and a regular coke. If you want to come out with me that's where I'll be. *[And he goes.]*

ALICE *is in a dilemma.*

ALICE: Oh god! What should I do? *[Turns to her* PASSENGERS *for help]* Is he worth it? Should I go out with him?

*[Again They respond overwhelmingly in the positive]*

EVERYBODY: Yairs...

ALICE: Oh, thanks, thank you. You are all simply the best passengers a connie could ever wish for. Sorry about the hassles and the yukkie stuff and all that that happened along the way, cause I just hope, despite all that ... I hope you all had a really really wonderful trip. So, see ya. *[She leaps off the tram, chasing after him]* Terry! Terry - wait...

*Out on the street she catches up with* TERRY, *they embrace and, holding hands run on into MacDonalds. The passengers disembark and* TRAN *drives the tram back to the depot.*

MORRIS STANLEY *was never seen again.*

THE END

## At the Malvern Depot Launch

Mayor Elaine Miller's champagne bottle smashes against the #938 and showers the Derro (Cliff Ellen) in alcohol. True to form Alice (Liz Sadler) cleans up.

Ruth Maddison shoots the cast

Alice (Liz Sadler) and fellow connies

# STORMING ST. KILDA BY TRAM REVIEWS

MAKING MIRTH ON THE MOVE:
...a uniquely Melbourne version of travelling theatre...this show (is) compulsive viewing. Some of the fun comes from the confusion between life and art. If you can drag your attention away from the drama inside the reactions of the passing motorists or genuine travellers trying to board constitute a comedy in themselves. Paul Davies has written a plot of sorts, but *Storming St, Kilda* relies on informality of pushing beyond the conventions of stage naturalism. There is no escape from the intimacy of public transport, and our private audience space is frequently invaded by actors playing all too familiar roles. In fact the characterization consists entirely of stereo-types, with much of the humour arising from the very predictability of their behavior. Alice the conductor is a battler with a heart of gold, Danny the Derro makes precisely the public nuisance of himself of which drunks have always been capable. You may not be much edified by Storming St. Kilda by Tram but you're bound to enjoy this robust slice of Melbourne life, an entirely appropriate offering for its Comedy Festival.
Helen Thomson *The Australian.*

WORTH GOING ALONG FOR THE RIDE:
I nervously boarded the tram outside Luna Park...and quietly prayed that the performance would not involve too much audience participation. The passengers – performing ones that is – range from a romantic punk to a film-making Sydney trendy in bad need of some primal therapy. There's an escort agency girl, an escapee from Brighton and of course a derro. The show has everything. Colour movement, travel sickness bags and an interval at Young and Jackson's.
Chris Boyd  *St. Kilda Times.*

BEST WEEKEND:
Melbourne's dynamic theatre scene provides drama for all tastes. TheatreWorks have staged works in unusual venues, including a hotel, a living room, and very successfully a tram. The company

mounts theatre of everyday life, encouraging audiences to think differently about the quality of their existence.
*Age Good Weekend Magazine 8/4/1988*

TRAM PLAY RUNS RIGHT ON TRACK:
Even the threat of a tram strike could not put this show off the track... the zany cast provided plenty of mayhem for the travelling audience...in what conductor Siobhan Tuke
*Herald Sun Melbourne 23/1/1991*

Melbourne's tramway system is one of the nine wonders of the world...something special also applies to the play *Storming St. Kilda By Tram*... The play captured the imagination of everyone who had ever ridden on the Met with its realism, wit and original lines.
*Western Independent 22/1/1991*

Melbourne's tramway system whether we like it or not is one of the major tourist attractions in our city, rain, hail or shine...and a first class conveyance for thousands of commuters everyday. The TheatreWorks group has jumped onto the tram bandwagon with a return season of *Storming St. Kilda By Tram*.

FUN NIGHT
The hilarious story unfolds as you travel along some of Melbourne's most scenic routes on Tram No 902 leaving at 8.17pm (sharp)... so buy your ticket early and some along for the ride of your life!
*Richmond Times i29/1/1991*

The most 'moving' piece of theatre you are ever likely to see is coming to a tram stop near you... Last performed three years ago Theatre Works *Storming St. Kilda By Tram* by award winning author Paul Davies is having a return season. Travel along some of Melbourne's most scenic routes in the Heart Health tram while enjoying some very funny theatre. Last performed three years ago *Storming St. Kilda* has been extensively revised, so if you've seen it before it will be well worth seeing again.
*Metro 30/1/1991*

...a thoroughly modern and uniquely Melbourne experience. TheatreWorks innovative show, *Storming St. Kilda By Tram* returns for a third triumphant season...performed on a moving Melbourne tram as it travels from St. Kilda to the city and back, it presents you with extraordinary stories of ordinary tram travellers. Trapped in a set of hilarious circumstances, their lives, and yours, as a result, will never be the same again.
*What's on in Melbourne* 4/2/1991

TRAM TO STORM ST. KILDA AGAIN
Trams. They provide a useful transport to and from a show. But a tram as the theatre? "Why not?" thought that highly imaginative company TheatreWorks back in 1983 and proceeded to stage a hit production *Storming Mont Albert By Tram*. Now its back with a script revised by author Paul Davies to make it even funnier.
*Coburg Courier* 5/2/1991


STORMING ST. KILDA
*Storming St. Kilda By Tram* the successor of the 1983 production *Storming Mont Albert By Tram* was one of the major hits of the 1988 Comedy Festival as it captured the imagination of everyone who has ever ridden on the Met ! The production sold out prior to opening night, and TheatreWorks has been inundated with requests ever since, and in 1989 *Storming St. Kilda By Tram* was awarded the AWGIE for "Best Community Theatre Piece of 1988"
*Collingwood City News* 5/2/1991

SHOW ON THE ROAD
...some of the most priceless moments as the action spills out of the tram between stops, are the looks on the faces of ordinary passers-by.
*Herald Sun*

ALL ABOARD FOR A RATTLING GOOD YARN OR TWO
It ran late of course and was packed but everyone aboard was smiling in a silly, expectant way. The connie was a sterling example of why they are indispensible. At the first stop a woman in black sequins boarded, she had been stranded when hubby had

skipped desert at Jean Jacques leaving her with only an Amex card. An old gent (fortified by more than public spirit) offered his last coins for the ride and the streetcar named desire lurched off at a cracking pace...after two hours we ended up back where we had started, but as the saying goes "to travel hopefully is a better thing than to arrive."
Rebecca Lancashire *The Age* 8/2/1991

BEST THEATRE
The highly acclaimed hit opened a return season with a revised script. It promises once more to be one of the most vigorous pieces of theatre in town.
*The Sunday Age* 10/2/1991

*STORMING ST. KILDA BY TRAM*
There is nothing like an unusual venue or setting to titillate the palate of the jaded theatre goer. *Storming St. Kilda By Tram* Melbourne's only perambulatory theatrical entertainment, has also returned for the third time, with a new cast and rewritten script. As with most truly successful ideas the premise is mouthwateringly simple. The audience join the tram in St. Kilda, which takes them via a circuitous route, into the city. Unlikely characters get on and off the tram at various stops, and the resultant interplay between them creates a lively and not too far removed from reality entertainment. The interval is observe d at Young and Jacksons and your ticket entitles you to a free beer. The plot strands are simple but engaging *Storming St. Kilda* is a mobile soap opera. *Storming St. Kilda* is a marvelous show with obviously limited seating that is worth booking ahead for. Much pleasure comes from when the drama spills over to the outside of the tram – when one character screams abuse of 'I love you' out of the door at another character at another who has alighted – because the expressions on the faces of the people on the street is absolutely priceless, indubitably the most fun you can have on the Met.
Fiona Scott-Norman 13/2/1991

## SOAP OPERA ON WHEELS

The latest incarnation of *Storming St. Kilda* has a new cast (Cliff Ellen excepted), several new gags and a different ending. Paul Davies has polished his script. His talent for one-liners gets better each year. "Time wounds all heels" an escort agency worker says to her jerk ex-boyfriend. Davies observations on contemporary society too, are getting more pungent and wryly perceptive. The ex-boyfriend for example, a chic filmmaker from Sydney talks of a course in group therapy which he took by correspondence. (Think about it!). In previous years I have complained that the scripts of these location theatre events have in general been underwritten and thus productions have relied too heavily on the environment. With this latest version of *Storming St. Kilda By Tram* the tram and the script are perfectly matched. The play couldn't exist without the location and vice versa. *Storming St. Kilda By Tram* is a soap-opera-buffa-cabaret on wheels. It will delight once a week theatre goers no less than the once a year punters. Do yourself a favour. Chris Boyd *The St. Kilda Times* 14/2/1991.

A young punk in St. Kilda proved reality is funnier than fiction when he tried to hitch a ride on a private tram used as the mobile venue for *Storming St. Kilda By Tram*. The unscheduled performance occurred when the tram stopped in Domain Rd. Sth Yarra to let one of the character actors on. The spikey-hired punk mistaking the vehicle for a real tram attempted to get on. The doors would not open for him so he hung on to the running board screaming "Let m in" until the next stop. Gaining entry he screamed abuse at the "conductor' and the audience, thinking he was part of the show laughed. The punk alighted at the next stop, commenting that he'd never ssen such a rude bunch. The audience of course applauded him.
*The Sunday Sun* 24/2/1991

A thoroughly enjoyable experience. The return of TheatreWorks' Awgie Award production allows the audience to laugh up a storm while *Storming St. Kilda By Tram* ... an extraordinary production as the venue is actually a mobile tram. This is by no means a conventional piece of theatre with scenes, props or intervals. Instead the audience adopts the role of passengers on the tram and the comedy/drama unfolds as the characters board the tram

from various terminals along the way. The success of this production lies in its recognition of all passengers' weakness: eavesdropping. *Storming St. Kilda By Tram* indulges our fondness for both eavesdropping and voyeurism with its colourful characters in their eye catching array. Forget about debating the benefits of buying a weekly ticket over a monthly one. Let me assure you, a ticket to *Storming St. Kilda By Tram* is the best value around.
Geraldine Doyle *Lot's Wife* 28/2/1991

TRAMS SNAKES AND TEA CAKES
One does not expect to find the words 'entertainment' and 'tram' in the same sentence. TheatreWorks current production *Storming St. Kilda By Tram* panders to the voyeur in us all, and does so with great humour and panache. *Storming St. Kilda By Tram* is one of a number of 'situational theatre' events being staged around Melbourne this summer, and these events require more active audience participation than does conventional theatre. The structure is developed around a series of incidents which unfold in front of the passengers/audience. These are actually short stories, moments in the lives of the characters who step aboard to participate in the comic-drama. The characters are primarily stereotypes, and Davies plays on the audience's prejudices, preconceptions and fantasies in order to demonstrate the pathos and humour of the human condition beneath the clichéd images they present to the world. The cast worked very hard to please and succeeded in most instances in providing very amusing characterizations. The timing of the production was very cleverly done, with the dramatic conclusion occurring just before the tram reached the terminus. Some of the most enjoyable moments in the play came from the reactions of people in traffic-bound adjacent cars, as one or two of the cast alighted from the tram and continued their antics on the footpath. Their reactions brought to mind Woody Allen's film *Stardust Memories.*
Paula Carr *Melbourne Report* (March 1991)

This wasn't your ordinary run-of-the-mill commuting journey. By courtesy of that innovative company TheatreWorks we were *Storming St. Kilda By Tram*. And after that any other trip would seem tame. So wholeheartedly do the actors enter into the spirit of

the thing that at first we looked askance at the seedy character sprawled on one of the seats, snoring loudly while a "tranny" blasted out the races. Then as the conductress tried to wake him up we realized that the play had begun. The script is easy on the intellect. Don't bother looking for a message, there isn't one. In all it's a couple of hours of relaxed good fun. It's easy to see why the original concept over in the eastern suburbs became almost a cult attraction, and why the St. Kilda version, launched in 1988 has been revived by genuine public demand.
Peg Morgan *Preston Post Times* 18/3/1991

# Worth going along for the ride

**STORMING ST. KILDA BY TRAM**
Theatreworks
(On The Number 69 Tram)
Departs St Kilda
Beach Tram Terminus
Until April 16
Review:
CHRIS BOYD

**COMEDY**

As a regular commuter on the Number 69 tram, I have been subjected to all kinds of weird behaviour.

Just yesterday morning I was accosted by a half-wit drunk with a bad case of halitosis and a tendency to froth at the mouth.

The tram conductor, who was wearing a Walkman at the time, was too busy doing a Michael Jackson *Beat It* impersonation to notice my screams for help.

On the tram home that evening the conductor sported two-tone Zig 'n' Zag lipstick – green and crimson – flame red hair, countless earrings and a pierced nose. She divided her time between terrifying elderly passengers and wiping her nose on her mittens.

Why, then, would I choose to review a comedy performance on a tram? Haven't I had enough experience of derros, punks, elephant men and psychopaths to last me a lifetime?

With this in mind, I nervously boarded the tram outside Luna Park, last Thursday evening, and quietly prayed that the performance would not involve too much audience participation.

Our "connie" for the night was Alice, new to the Metropolitan Transit Authority. Alice is personable, but unusually obsessed with the cleaning of her tram. She packs a bottle of *Spray and Wipe*, a swag of *Chux Super Wipes*, and a Kambrook portable vacuum cleaner.

The passengers performing ones, that is – range from a romantic punk to a film-making Sydney trendy badly in need of some primal therapy.

There's an escort agency girl ("Concession, please"), an escapee from Brighton (who thinks that a 7-11 is a sort of cologne) and, of course, a derro.

This show has everything. Colour, movement, scenery, travel sickness bags, and an interval at Chloe's (upstairs and *Underage and Jackson's*) where the audience is feted for half an hour.

Danny the Derro (otherwise known as Cliff Ellen) samples the Great Australian Dinner just where the connie told him not to during the portable show Storming St Kilda By Tram. Phot: RUTH MADDISON.

# All aboard for a rattling good yarn or two

**REPORT**
**REBECCA LANCASHIRE**

THERE'S no better place to be a fly on the wall than in a tram. It's like mobile living-room rattling through the night, with strangers acting out domestic dilemmas en route. For $1.60 you can hear all about births, deaths, marriages and why Collingwood has been on a winning streak since 1937.

Then there was the time an elderly man, after staring at me from Williamstown to Footscray, stood up and announced to the rest of the carriage that I had moonlighted as Natalie Wood in 'Splendor in the Grass' (1961). It's rumored that certain writers travel the Met eavesdropping for inspiration, and last night's 8.27 pm from St Kilda would have produced a novella or two.

It ran late, of course, and was packed, but everyone aboard was smiling in a silly, expectant way. The connie was a sterling example of why they are indispensible. She kept herself busy vacuuming and squirting Windowlene and confessed she was turned on by trams; it was something to do with their wooden interiors, she said. Ms Kitramski obviously took pride in her work-station; there was even a plastic rose air-freshener stuck on the window.

At the first stop, a woman in black sequins boarded. Unaccustomed as she was to public transport, she had been stranded when hubby had skipped dessert at Jean Jacques leaving her with only an Amex card. Unfortunately the Met preferred loose change. An old gent (fortified by more than public spirit) offered his last coins for the ride and the streetcar named desire lurched off at a cracking pace.

"Time wounds all heels, Ni[g]" screeched a young woman in yellow to her gormless companion. A punk ca[n] Terry confessed his lust for the con[duc]tress, who locked herself and her fe[ath]er duster in the driver's compartm[ent] Somewhere along the line a pla[y] guide-dog got a ticket to ride and we hadn't reached South Yarra.

By the time we turned into Swan[ston] Street, and those aboard No. 902 wer[e at] crisis point, a ticket inspector turned [up.] He promptly ordered all passenger[s off] and into a pub to recover. After [two] hours we ended up back where we started, but as the saying goes: "To [trav]el hopefully is a better thing tha[n to] arrive".

Theatreworks' 'Storming St Kilda [by] Tram' departs Monday to Saturda[y at] 8.27 pm sharp from the St Kilda B[each] Terminus opposite Luna Park for a [lim]ited season. Bookings: 650 1500 BASS. Inquiries: 534 4879.

---

*All aboard while smoking a cigarette, is the call during the play Storming St Kilda by Tram, at the St Kilda Terminus, which starts on Friday February 1.*

MELBOURNE'S tramway system, is one of the nine wonders of the world, according to local and overseas commuters who regard it as something special.

Something special also applies to the play *Storming St Kilda by Tram*, which starts its season on Friday February 1. The play will be staged on a tram which departs the St Kilda terminus, cnr Ackland and Upper Esplanade, St Kilda Monday to Saturday at 8.27pm. It is being produced under the guidance of the Theatreworks Group.

Spokeswoman Georgie Howitt said the play captured the imagination of everyone who had ever ridden on the Met with its realism, wit and original lines.

She said theatregoers would be able to see the production while travelling along some of the most scenic routes on the National Heart Foundation tram.

The cast includes outer fringe members, Siobhan Tuke, Cliff Ellen, Sally-Anne Upton, Carole Patullo, Louis Dingemans and Taya Straton.

# Making mirth on the move

**Theatre**

**Storming St Kilda by Tram**
by Paul Davies
Theatreworks
Melbourne

## HELEN THOMSON

THIS is the second time Theatreworks have set off in a green rattler to entertain the public with a uniquely Melbourne version of travelling theatre. Six years ago they did a show called *Storming Mont Albert by Tram* and they have now come up with a new version as part of Melbourne's Comedy Festival.

If ever you've whiled away the commuting hours musing or fantasising about your fellow travellers' real lives, then this show will be compulsive viewing. Some of the fun comes from the genuine confusion between life and art. If you can drag your attention away from the drama inside, the reactions of passing motorists or genuine travellers trying to board constitute a comedy in themselves.

Paul Davies has written a plot of sorts, but *Storming St Kilda* relies on informality, on pushing beyond the conventions of stage naturalism. There is no escape from the intimacy of public transport, and our private audience space is frequently invaded by actors playing all too familiar roles.

In fact the characterisation consists entirely of stereotypes, with much of the humour arising from the very predictability of their behaviour. Alice the conductor is a battler with a heart of gold, Danny the Derro makes precisely the public nuisance of himself of which drunks have always been capable.

When Cathy and Nigel accidentally meet after parting 14 years earlier and throw the normal inhibitions of public behaviour to the winds, we eavesdrop avidly. The anti-social Terry, complete with manic laugh and lots of black leather, is quite terrifyingly familiar.

As theatre it's all pretty basic and familiar. The second half never does live up to the promise of the first, but it's nevertheless made enjoyable by the tram ride itself and the sense that any tram ride might well contain the possibility of such drama or throw up similarly uninhibited characters and behaviour.

Director Mark Shiffcis has got together an excellent cast who tackle their roles, with both conviction and gusto. I particularly liked Jeremy Stanford's Terry, so locked into the reflex responses of the punk we never were sure whether he was sane, drugged or daft.

Peter Finlay deteriorated from yuppie assurance to primal screaming (he has a teddy bear in his briefcase) with his pretensions satisfyingly exploded.

You may not be much edified by *Storming St Kilda by Tram*, but you're bound to enjoy this robust slice of Melbourne life, an entirely appropriate offering for its Comedy Festival.

# TheatreWorks are Storming St Kilda by Tram

## Peg Morgan's Spotlight

SOME of us are gluttons for punishment.

You would think that a weekday journey to work from Melbourne's south east to its Far North involving two different trams with all its delays would be enough.

But there was I, waiting at a St Kilda stop for yet another - and on a Saturday afternoon, what's more.

However, this wasn't your ordinary run-of-the-mill, commuting journey. By courtesy of that innovative company TheatreWorks, we were *Storming St Kilda by Tram*.

And after that, any other trip would seem tame.

Now based in St Kilda, the company has recreated in its new location the formula established so successful-ly in 1983 with *Storming Mont Albert by Tram*.

First, they charter one green "boneshaker" on the St Kilda-City route, then fill it with ordinary passengers (the audience) spiced with eight who are anything but ordinary (the cast.)

So wholeheartedly do the actors enter into the spirit of the thing that at first we looked askance at the seedy character sprawled on one of the seats, snoring loudly while a "tranny" blasted out the races.

Then, as the conductress tried to wake him up we realised that the play had begun, with Danny O'Rourke, self-proclaimed political scientist and turf consultant, played by Cliff Ellen, and Sioban Tuke as "Connie" Allce.

New characters boarded at almost every stop, ranging from Samantha Hart-Byrne, the yuppy Brighton housewife played by Carole Patullo, , to Terry the Punk (Louis Dingemans),.

Others were escort agency worker Kathy (Taya Straton) and her former lover, film-maker Nigel (Jon Cancannon), re-united by chance on the tram; an officious ticket inspector (Roger Selleck) and a policewoman (Sally-Anne Upton).

Some alighted (or were ejected) on the way into the city and were greeted like the old friends they had become when they re-joined the tram on the way home.

Meanwhile we audi-ence members had paid our respects to Chloe at No 1, Swanston St, while enjoying complimentary drinks.

(Hard to believe that this was the first time my friend and I, both Melbourne-born, had met the famous lady "in the flesh." But for many years, this was strictly male territory)

Director Mark Shirrefs, on his third *Storming* expedition, is now also associated with *Lawyers, Guns and Money*.

The script written by Paul Davies is laid-back and easy on the intellect. Don't bother looking for the message - there isn't one.

Gags are mostly topical, like the reference to the man who lost his money in the "Sarcophagus" Building Society.

In all, it's a couple of hours of relaxed good fun. It's easy to see why the original concept over in the eastern suburbs became almost a cult attraction, and why the St Kilda version, launched in 1988, has been revived by genuine public demand.

This very special tram leaves from the St Kilda Beach terminus (opposite Luna Park) Mondays to Saturdays at 3.27 sharp, with Saturday matinees at 4.27pm.

Booking essential, on 650 1500 amd BASS, further information from TheatreWorks on 534 4879.

# Tram to storm St Kilda again

TRAMS. They provide useful transport to and from a show. But a tram as the theatre?

"Why not?" thought that highly-imaginative company TheatreWorks, back in 1983, and proceeded to stage a hit production, *Storming Mont Albert by Tram* on one of the good old green rollers.

When they moved to the southern suburbs, it was a matter of writing a new script, changing the route and they had *Storming St Kilda by Tram*.

This proved one of the great successes of the 1988 Comedy Festival, selling out before opening night and gaining the Best Community Theatre Piece award.

Now, it's back with the script revised by author Paul Davies to make it even funnier.

Mark Shirrefs, directing his third "Tram Show", has assembled one of the most talented comedy casts.

The travellers meet Siobhan Tuke as the hapless conductress; Carole Patullo as Samantha Heart-Byrne the socialite; Louis Dingemans (Terry the Punk) and John Concannon as Nigel Davidson the Sydney film-maker.

There's a ticket inspector of course, played by Roger Selleck, and a policewoman, portrayed by Sally-Anne Upton.

Others in the cast are Taya Straton, and Cliff Ellnn.

Describing it as "a moving piece of theatre", the company promises patrons "the ride of their lives".

The Tram leaves the St Kilda Beach terminus (opposite Luna Park) at 8.27 pm Mondays to Saturdays, with a 4.27 pm matinee also on Saturdays. Inquiries to TheatreWorks, 534 4879; bookings on 650 1500 and BASS.

DANDENONG EXAMINER

Date.... 19 FEB 1991

## Theatre

BY popular demand, Theatreworks is currently presenting a return season of "Storming St Kilda by Tram" which was a major hit during the 1988 Melbourne Comedy Festival, as it captured the imagination of everyone who has ever ridden on the Met!

Author, Paul Davies, has revised the script, moving "The Tram Show" into the nineties. Some of the best comedy cast in Melbourne has been assembled including Siobhan Tuke, a regular

Comedy Company folk, Carole Patullo, Cliff Ellen and Roger Selleck.

The hilarious story unfolds as you travel along some of Melbourne's most scenic routes on tram No 902, leaving at 8.17pm sharp from Acland Street Terminus.

Already the first week is sold out and it is only limited season. There is Saturday matinee a 4.27pm. For bookings phone 650-1500 or Bas

ESSENDON MOONEE PONDS NORTHERNER

Date... 20 FEB 1991

Cast members from the riotous production "Storming St Kilda By Tram" now in a brand new season on a tram leaving Acland Street Terminus opposite Luna Park Monday to Saturdays at 8.17 pm sharp. Marvellous experience you should not miss. Book on 650 1500 and tell 'em

# VIC HEALTH IS KEEPING THEATRE ON THE RIGHT TRACK.

Not all plays are trapped by the limits of the stage. Sometimes they escape into the street, breathing new life into old ways and theatre everywhere benefits from the exercise.

Which is why it seems very appropriate that Theatreworks' bold production of 'Storming St Kilda by Tram' is sponsored by Vic Health on behalf of the National Heart Foundation's Heart Health Campaign. It's a trip we're happy to take.

For more information about Vic Health's funding programme, call (03) 347 3777

HEART HEALTH
FUNDED BY THE VICTORIAN HEALTH FOUNDATION FOR THE NATIONAL HEART FOUNDATION

HERALD-SUN
Melbourne

Date.... -7 FEB 1991

## Show on the road

OVER in Luna Park land, the zany crowd from TheatreWorks present a return season of their huge hit, *Storming St Kilda by Tram.*

The show, performed aboard a tram which loops around various Melbourne tram routes (with a watering break at Young & Jackson's Hotel in the city), is a great night of spontaneous comedy.

The characters, including a drunken hobo, a menacing young punk, a lost Yuppie, a tramways inspector, a hapless conductor and a very enthusiastic member of the Victoria Police, engage in a madcap plot of arguments, fisticuffs, love and intrigue.

But some of the most priceless moments, as the action spills out of the tram between stops, are the looks on the faces of ordinary passers-by.

● Terry Meagher plays punk Louis Dingemans with Roger Sellect as Inspector Stanley.

● Off the rails ... the zany cast of *Storming St Kilda By Tram.*

## Tram play runs right on track

EVEN the threat of a tram strike could not put this show off track.

The opening performance of Theatreworks' *Storming St Kilda By Tram* went ahead as planned yesterday — without any chaos in the transport industry.

But the zany cast provided plenty of mayhem for the travelling audience.

Sponsored by the National Heart Foundation, *Storming St Kilda By Tram* is a satirical journey from the St Kilda beach terminus to the city, with an interval at Young and Jackson's hotel.

Theatre-goers can join a punk, policewoman, Brighton socialite, Sydney film-maker and ticket inspector in what conductor Siobhan Tuke described as "an everyday wacky trip on the Met with weirdo commuters".

Characters embark and disembark along a scenic route to entertain an unsuspecting audience.

Ms Tuke said the play's creativity and unusual venue were its highlights.

Tickets are $29.50 adults and $19.40 concession.

Discounts apply for group bookings.

IN-PRESS

Date: 13 FEB 1991

## STORMING ST KILDA BY TRAM
## Luna Park Tram Stop, Tram No 902

As the various producers of the recent spate of 'garden' plays are well aware, there is nothing like an unusual venue or setting to titillate the palate of the jaded theatre-goer; Loving Friends extended their season until February 14th, Wind In The Willows has been going for five years, and even Theatresports are launching their new season in the Botanical Gardens. Storming St Kilda By Tram, Melbourne's only perambulatory theatrical entertainment, has also returned for the third time, with a new cast and re-written script.

As with most truly successful ideas, the premise is mouthwateringly simple. The audience join the tram in St Kilda, which takes them, via a circuitous route, into the city. Unlikely characters get on and off the tram at various stops, and the resultant interplay between them creates a lively and not too far removed from reality entertainment. The interval is observed at Young and Jacksons, and your ticket entitles you to a free beer.

The plot strands are simple but engaging: Storming St Kilda is a mobile soap opera. The acting is all excellent, especially Louis Dingemans (former Cabbage Brother), as the appealing punk who falls in love with the Conductor (Sioban Tuke). From the moment he explodes onto the tram clutching a stolen plastic dog, he dominates the show. Also notable are Taya Straton as she stoically fends off the attentions of her yuppy ex-boyfriend who has reappeared after a nine-year absence, and Carole Patullo as the snotty society woman who couldn't find a taxi.

Storming St Kilda is a marvellous show with obviously limited seating that is worth booking ahead for. Much pleasure comes from when the drama spills over to the outside of the tram — when one character screams abuse or 'I love you' out of the door at another who has alighted — because the expressions on the faces of people on the street is absolutely priceless. Indubitably the most fun you can have on the Met.

★ Fiona Scott-Norman

# Taking a different look at tram travel

TRAMS. They provide useful transport to and from a show. But a tram as the theatre?

"Why not" thought that highly imaginative company Theatre Works back in 1983, and staged a hit production *Storming Mont Albert by Tram* on one of the good old green rollers.

When the group moved south, it was just a matter of writing a new script and changing the route — and they had *Storming St Kilda by Tram*.

This proved one of the great successes of the 1988 Comedy Festival, selling out to eager patrons before opening night, and gaining an award for the Best Community Theatre Piece of the year.

Now, it's back by genuine demand, with the script revised by author Paul Davies to make it funnier than ever.

Mark Shirrefs, directing his third "Tram Show" has assembled one of the most talented comedy casts in Melbourne.

The travellers meet Siobhan Tuke as the hapless conductress, Carole Patullo as Samantha Heart-Byrne the Brighton socialite, Louis Dingemans (Terry the Punk) and John Concannon as Nigel Davidson the Sydney film-maker.

There's a ticket inspector of course, played by Roger Selleck, and a policewoman, portrayed by Sally-Anne Upton.

Others in the cast are Taya Straton, and Cliff Ellen.

Describing it as "a moving piece of theatre", the company promises patrons "the ride of their lives".

The tram leaves the St Kilda Beach Terminus (opposite Luna Park) at 8.27 pm Mondays to Saturdays, with a 4.27 pm matinee on Saturdays.

Bookings are essential. Inquiries to Theatre Works, 534 4879; bookings on 650 1500 and BASS.

# STORMING ST. KILDA BY TRAM

I'll let you in on a little secret — travelling by public transport can be a thoroughly enjoyable experience. That is, of course, if you catch the 8.27pm tram from the St Kilda Beach terminal opposite Luna Park.

The return of Theatrework's Awgie Award production allows the audience to laugh up a storm while **Storming St Kilda by Tram**. Storming St Kilda by Tram, is an extraordinary production, as the venue is actually a mobile tram which makes a return trip to the City from St Kilda (via Young and Jackson's for a free drink!).

This is by no means a conventional piece of theatre with scenes, props or intervals. Instead, the audience adopts the role of passengers on the tram, and the comedy/drama unfolds as characters board the tram from the various terminals along the way.

The success of this production lies in its recognition of all passengers' weakness: eavesdropping. As the most seasoned passengers know, it is always the lure of another person's newspaper or the snippets of their conversation which enlivens a dull journey. Storming St Kilda by Tram indulges our fondness for both eavesdropping and voyeurism with its colourful characters in their eyecatching array.

On tram number 902, your journey will be punctuated by the witty insults exchanged between the mismatched pair of Cathy and Nigel, and you will delight in the trials and tribulations of Samantha Heart-Byrne. Any of your political queries will be quickly sorted out by Danny O'Rourke, a philosopher of sorts who is fond of the odd drink, and no doubt you will fumble for y ticket when the ticket inspec boards the tram. You'll see t love blossom before your ey and your feet will start tapp when Senior Constable Kro launches into a blues numt shaking the full weight of the up and down the tram.

Having 'Stormed St Kilda Tram', I urge you to forget ab debating the benefits of buyin weekly ticket over a monthly o Let me assure you, a ticket Storming St Kilda by Tram is best value around.

Theatreworks' Storming Kilda by Tram departs 8.27 Monday to Saturday from the Kilda Beach terminal oppos Luna Park. Bookings, ring 6 1500 or Bass. Enquiries, r 534 4879. Runs for a limit season only.

*by Geraldine D*

## · THEATRE ·

# Trams, snakes and tea-cake

• PAULA CARR •

ONE does not expect to find the words 'entertainment' and 'tram' in the same sentence. On those long, seemingly endless journeys through Melbourne on the 'green rattlers' the traveller either drifts into introspection or otherwise casts voyeuristic glances over their fellow commuters and listens to their conversations. Where is that old lady going? Are the young man and the pretty girl in the next seat lovers? Friends? Siblings? Why are they fighting? Why is that man carrying a TV aerial and a woman's sun hat? Will that pregnant woman have twins?

TheatreWorks' current production *Storming St Kilda by Tram* written by Paul Davies and directed by Mark Shirrefs, panders to the voyeur in us all, and does so with great humour and panache. The entertainment takes place aboard a tram journeying from St Kilda to Young and Jacksons' Hotel then back to St Kilda. At the Ackland Street terminus the audience is invited aboard by a sassy tram 'connie' Alice Katranski (played by the effervescent Sioban Tuke) and you just know that it is going to be an eventful trip. Safety procedures are outlined — as they are on airplanes — and we are away, skimming (or should that be storming?) through the Melbourne night.

*Storming* is one of a number of 'situational theatre' events being staged around Melbourne this summer, and these events require more active audience participation than does conventional theatre. The structure of *Storming* is developed around a series of incidents which unfold in front of the passengers/ audience, (who occasionally get drawn into the fracas, due to the proximity of the audience to the action). These incidents are in actuality short stories, moments in the lives of the characters who step aboard to participate in the comic-drama.

The characters are primarily stereotypes, and Davies plays on the audience's prejudices, preconceptions and fantasies in order to demonstrate the pathos and humour of the human condition beneath the cliched images they present to the world. There is Danny O'Rourke (played by the laconic Cliff Ellen) a bit of a bum and an inveterate gambler who relies on his experiences as a war veteran for credibility. He has taken up more or less permanent residence on the tram, to the disgust of Samantha Heart-Byrn a pretentious Brighton matron who is on her way to the Opera. Samantha (Carole Patullo) attired in the mandatory 'little black dress,' experiencing marital problems, and sipping champagne from a flute glass, is a snooty rich twit who accuses O'Rourke of being a parasite. The irony is apparent.

Nigel Davidson, well groomed yuppie (what are all these rich folk doing catching trams?) and archetypal con artist, is unexpectedly confronted with his ex-girlfriend, Cathy Waterman, who has coincidentally caught the same tram. Cathy has not experienced the same financial success as Nigel the corporate promotions whiz, indeed she is now employed in the 'oldest profession!' Nigel (Jon Concannon) and Cathy (Taya Straton) are the most developed, and thus the most interesting characters in the production and their encounter brings forth many surprises, both for themselves and for the audience.

Terry Meagher (Louis Dingemans) is the punk we all dread to encounter late at night. Brash and belligerent, dressed to kill in slashed black clobber, and armed with a Lady Nell plastic dog, Terry is a delight. He fulfils the audience's fantasies of being mugged-raped-murdered on public transport but his story, not surprisingly, has an unexpected twist when he falls for Alice the 'connie.'

The last two characters in the production are Morris Stanley (Roger Selleck), the raincoated tram inspector with a penchant for illuminated bow ties and the larger-than-life Snr Constable Wendy Kroger (convincingly played by Sally-Anne Upton).

The cast worked very hard to please and succeeded in most instances in providing very amusing characterizations. The timing of the production was very cleverly done, with the dramatic conclusion occurring just before the tram reached the terminus. The sound, however, caused minor problems when characters occasionally faced away from some of the audience (an inevitable occurrence due to the confined space of the tram). Voices competed for attention with the background noise of traffic.

Some of the most enjoyable moments in the play came from the reactions of people in traffic-bound adjacent cars, as one or two of the cast alighted from the tram and continued their antics on the footpath. Their reactions brought to mind Woody Allen's film *Stardust Memories*, where Allen is on a stationary train filled with morose uncommunicative, mundane passengers. Glancing across the railway platform he sees a second train in which a party is in full swing. The passengers are drinking champagne, streamers are everywhere, there is music, laughter, and a beautiful woman is blowing kisses through the glass. He cannot, however, get off his train to join the party. The responses of the car-bound observers were much like Allen's. The tram no doubt looked a lot more fun than their own solitary journeys, and from their reactions a number of the autophiles would have liked to abandon their vehicles and join us on our odyssey, as we stormed inexorably towards St Kilda.

MELBOURNE REPORT

THE MELBOURNE TIMES

Date........................ 20 FEB 1991

AS TheatreWorks enters its second decade, it is about to embark upon the third phase of its history.

When founded, in 1980, the company went about providing Melbourne's Eastern suburbs with community theatre. Five years later, TheatreWorks relocated to Acland Street in St Kilda where it has become a near indispensable part of the local bohemian spirit.

This latest return season of *Storming St Kilda By Tram*, one of the company's earliest and most enduring works, marks the end of TheatreWorks as we know it. The first time the show was mounted, the destination was Mont Albert. The cast for that first production reads like a who's who of TheatreWorks: Paul Davies, Caz Howard, Peter Sommerfield, Peter Finlay and Hannie Rayson.

Following Paul Davies' resignation, late last year, Robert Draffin has been appointed as TheatreWorks' artistic director.

Draffin, one of this country's most gifted directors, will quite literally transform the company. It is an exciting and unexpected move by the TheatreWorks board. More information on the company's new direction should be available in coming weeks.

The latest incarnation of *Storming St Kilda* has a new cast (Cliff Ellen excepted) several new gags and a different ending. Paul Davies has polished his script. His talent for one-liners gets better each year! "Time wounds all heels," an escort agency worker's says to her jerk ex-boyfriend.

Davies' observations on contemporary society, too, are getting more pungent and wryly perceptive. The ex-boyfriend, for example, a chic "filmmaker" from Sydney, talks of a course in group therapy he took by correspondence. (Think about it!).

In previous years, I have complained that the scripts of these location-theatre events have, in general, been underwritten and thus productions have relied too heavily on the environment. With this latest version of *Storming St Kilda*, with tram and the script are perfectly matched. The play couldn't exist without the location – and vice versa.

*Storming St Kilda by Tram* is a soap-opera-buffa-cabaret on wheels. It will delight once-a-week theatregoers no less than once-a-year punters. Do yourself a favour......

# ARENA

## WHAT'S ON AND WHERE

THE most 'moving' piece of theatre you are ever likely to see is coming to a tram stop near you.

TheatreWorks' 'Storming St Kilda By Tram', by award winning author Paul Davies, is having a return season. Travel along some of Melbourne's most scenic routes in the Heart Health tram while enjoying some very funny theatre.

Last performed three years ago, 'Storming St Kilda' has been extensively revised, so if you've seen it before, it will be well worth seeing again. The cast includes Siobhan Tuke as the hapless conductress, Carole Patullo as Brighton socialite Samantha Heart-Byrne, Louis Dingemans as Terry the punk, and Sally-Anne Upton as the policewoman.

'Storming St Kilda By Tram' runs from February 1 for a limited season. The Heart Health tram departs from the St Kilda Beach Terminus, opposite Luna Park, at 8.27pm Mondays to Fridays with a Saturday matinee tram leaving at 4.27pm. Bookings are essential. Call 650 1500 or Bass.

WERRIBEE Park, historic home of the wealthy colonial 'wool king' Thomas Chirnside, has special attractions throughout the summer. Entertainment every Sunday includes a variety of colonial games for children, music, singing, Scottish piping, and croquet exhibitions in which visitors can participate.

Enjoy a stroll through Victoria's State Rose Garden. Laid out in the shape of a giant

All aboard for 'Storming St Kilda B Tram'.

Tudor rose, the garden covers five hectares and contains more than 4,500 roses of 150 varieties now in full bloom.

There are also formal gardens and Mary Chirnside's elaborate grotto on the lake, decorated with shell and pebbles, where the butler used to serve her afternoon tea a hundred years ago.

Werribee Park Mansion has a new attraction, a Victorian 'scrap screen', recently donated from a private collection. The four panel screen consists of hundreds of intricately arranged paper cut-outs of flowers, birds, landscapes, animals and people. One side depicts the four seasons while the other features scenes of family life within wreaths and garlands of flowers.

Cassell's 'Household Guide' of 1877 recommended that "Preparing scraps with which to cover a screen is an employment that fills up a good deal of spare time, entails no mental exertion and may be done at small expense."

If you feel like imitating upper class Victorian young ladies, reproduction Victorian scraps are available at Werribee Park for 1990s homemakers.

Entry to Werribee Park is free. Admission to the mansion costs $3.60 adults, $1.80 child/pensioner and $10.50 family.

IF you have any cash left over from all that Christmas spending and are something of a car fanatic, Christie's are holding a sale of autojumble — cars, antiques and private memorabilia from a private museum at Echuca.

The Alambee Auto and Folk Museum houses an extraordinary collection of vintage and veteran cars, motor cycles, buses, trucks, bicycles, early gramophones, sewing machines, bottles and early tools and household items.

A highlight of the collection of lovingly restored cars is a Crossley touring car, used for the Prince of Wales on a visit to Australia in the 1920s.

For further information contact Paul Sumner on 820 4311 or Norman Simmons, Museum owner and curator on (054) 82 3653.

# TheatreWorks are Storming St Kilda by Tram

## Peg Morgan's Spotlight

SOME of us are gluttons for punishment.

You would think that a weekday journey to work from Melbourne's south east to its Far North involving two different trams with all its delays would be enough.

But there was I, waiting at a St Kilda stop for yet another - and on a Saturday afternoon, what's more.

However, this wasn't your ordinary run-of-the-mill, commuting journey. By courtesy of that innovative company TheatreWorks, we were *Storming St Kilda by Tram*.

And after that, any other trip would seem tame.

Now based in St Kilda, the company has recreated in its new location the formula established so successfully in 1983 with *Storming Mont Albert by Tram*.

First, they charter one green "boneshaker" on the St Kilda-City route, then fill it with ordinary passengers (the audience) spiced with eight who are anything but ordinary (the cast.)

So wholeheartedly do the actors enter into the spirit of the thing that at first we looked askance at the seedy character sprawled on one of the seats, snoring loudly while a "tranny" blasted out the races.

Then, as the conductress tried to wake him up we realised that the play had begun, with Danny O'Rourke, self-proclaimed political scientist and turf consultant, played by Cliff Ellen, and Sioban Tuke as "Connie" Alice.

New characters boarded at almost every stop, ranging from Samantha Hart-Byrne, the yuppy Brighton housewife played by Carole Patullo, , to Terry the Punk (Louis Dingemans),.

Others were escort agency worker Kathy (Taya Straton) and her former lover, film-maker Nigel (Jon Cancannon), re-united by chance on the tram; an officious ticket inspector (Roger Selleck) and a policewoman (Sally-Anne Upton).

Some alighted (or were ejected) on the way into the city and were greeted like the old friends they had become when they rejoined the tram on the way home.

Meanhile we audience members had paid our respects to Chloe at No 1, Swanston St, while enjoying complimentary drinks.

(Hard to believe that this was the first time my friend and I, both Melbourne-born, had met the famous lady "in the flesh." But for many years, this was strictly male territory)

Director Mark Shirrefs, on his third *Storming* expedition, is now also associated with *Lawyers, Guns and Money*.

The script written by Paul Davies is laid-back and easy on the intellect. Don't bother looking for the message - there isn't one.

Gags are mostly topical, like the reference to the man who lost his money in the "Sarcophagus" Building Society.

In all, it's a couple of hours of relaxed good fun. It's easy to see why the original concept over in the eastern suburbs became almost a cult attraction, and why the St Kilda version, launched in 1988, has been revived by genuine public demand.

This very special tram leaves from the St Kilda Beach terminus (opposite Luna Park) Mondays to Saturdays at 8.27 sharp, with Saturday matinees at 4.27pm.

Booking essential, on 650 1500 amd BASS, further information from TheatreWorks on 534 4879.

PRESTON POST TIMES

11 FEB 1991

# Patrons will get 'the ride of their lives'

TRAMS. They provide useful transport — to and from a show. But a tram as the theatre?

"Why not" thought that highly imaginative company Theatre Works back in 1983, and proceeded to stage a hit production *Storming Mont Albert by Tram* on one of the good old green rollers.

When the group moved to the southern suburbs, it was just a matter of writing a new script and changing the route — and they had *Storming St Kilda by Tram*.

Now, it's back by genuine demand, with the script revised by author Paul Davies to make it funnier.

Mark Shirrefs, directing his third "Tram Show" has assembled one of the most talented comedy casts in Melbourne.

The travellers meet Siobhan Tuke as the hapless conductress; Carole Patullo as Samantha Heart-Byrne the Brighton socialite; Louis Dingemans (Terry the Punk) and John Concannon as Nigel Davidson the Sydney film-maker, among others.

Describing it as "a moving piece of theatre" the company promises patrons "the ride of their lives".

The 'Tram' leaves the St Kilda Beach Terminus (opposite Luna Park) at 8.27 pm Mondays to Saturdays, with a 4.27 pm matinee also on Saturdays.

However, booking is essential. All inquiries to Theatre Works on 534 4879; bookings on 650 1500 and BASS.

### STORMING ST. KILDA

"Storming St. Kilda By Tram", the successor of the 1983 production "Storming Mont Albert By Tram" was one of the major hits of the 1988 Melbourne Comedy Festival, as it captured the imagination of everyone who has ever ridden on the Met!

The production sold out prior to opening night, and Theatre Works has been inundated with requests ever since, and in 1989 "Storming St. Kilda By tram" was awarded a AWGIE for "Best Community Theatre Piece 1988".

### INTO THE NINETIES

Author, Paul Davies, has substantially revised the script, moving "The Tram Show" into the nineties.

Mark Shirrefs, the director, has again gathered together one of the most talented comedy casts in Melbourne, including Siobhan Tuke, Carole Patullo, Sally-Anne Upton, Louis Dingemans, Taya Straton, Cliff Ellen and Roger Selleck.

### FUN NIGHT

The hilarious story unfolds as you travel along some of Melbourne's most scenic routes on Tram No. 902, leaving at 8.17pm (sharp) from Acland Street Terminus. "Storming St. Kilda By Tram" is guaranteed to sell quickly so buy your ticket early and come along for the ride of your life!

### HAIL CARS HERE

"Storming St. Kilda" began its new season on February 1st.

RICHMOND CITY NEWS

Date 12 FEB 1991

Cast members from the riotous production "Storming St Kilda By Tram" now in a brand new season on a tram leaving Acland Street Terminus opposite Luna Park Monday to Saturdays at 8.17 pm sharp. Marvellous experience you should not miss. Book on 650 1500 and tell 'em Pete sent you.

● "Don't listen to them Rover. Of course you're allowed on the tram!" says Louis Dingemans at the *Storming St Kilda By Tram* party.

Date: 14 FEB 1991

## Arts and Entertainment

# Soap opera on wheels

STORMING ST KILDA BY TRAM.
By Paul Davies
Theatreworks
Review: CHRIS BOYD

### THEATRE

As TheatreWorks enters its second decade, it is about to embark upon the third phase of its history.

When founded, in 1980, the company went about providing Melbourne's Eastern suburbs with community theatre. Five years later, TheatreWorks relocated to Acland Street in St Kilda where it has become a near indispensable part of the local bohemian spirit.

This latest return season of Storming St Kilda By Tram, one of the company's earliest and most enduring works, marks the end of TheatreWorks as we know it. The first time the show was mounted, the destination was Mont Albert. The cast for that first production reads like a who's who of Theatre-Works: Paul Davies, Caz Howard, Peter Sommerfield, Peter Finlay and Hannie Rayson.

Following Paul Davies' resignation, late last year, Robert Draffin has been appointed as Theatre-Works' artistic director.

Draffin, one of this country's most gifted directors, will quite literally transform the company. It is an exciting and unexpected move by the TheatreWorks board. More information on the company's new direction should be available in coming weeks.

The latest incarnation of Storming St Kilda has a new cast (Cliff Ellen excepted), several new gags and a different ending. Paul Davies has polished his script. His talent for one-liners gets better each year! "Time wounds all heels," an escort agency worker's

Pictures: PETER WEAVING

Storming St Kilda by Tram and tramming up a storm: the TheatreWorks cast whoops it up on wheels.

Davies' observations on contemporary society, too, are getting more pungent and wryly perceptive. The ex-boyfriend, for example, a chic "filmmaker" from Sydney talks of a course by correspondence. (Think about it!)

In previous years, I have complained that the scripts of these location-theatre events have, in general, been underwritten — have relied too heavily on the environment. With this latest version of Storming St Kilda, with tram and the script are perfectly matched. The play couldn't exist without the

Storming St Kilda by Tram is a soap-opera buffa-cabaret on wheels. It will delight once-a-week theatregoers no less than once-a-year punters.

THE SUNDAY AGE
Melbourne

Date.......... 1 0 FEB 1991

## BEST THEATRE

The highly acclaimed hit from the 1988 Comedy Festival, the **TheatreWorks'** production of '**Storming St Kilda By Tram**', opened a return season in Melbourne on Friday. With a revised script by author, **Paul Davies**, it promises once more to be one of the most vigorous pieces of theatre in town. The tram itself leaves from the St Kilda beach terminus opposite Luna Park, Monday to Saturday 8.27 pm, with a Saturday matinee at 4.27 pm.

# The law is a miserable ass

LAWYERS have been warned not to say "good morning" to judges in court. The latest *Law Society Bulletin* warns that visitors to court may think lawyers are on over-familiar terms with the judiciary if the cheery greeting is used.

A Melbourne legal eagle said the warning was "essentially correct" but unlikely to be heeded in some courts.

"Some of the old darlings on the bench like a chat and brief bit of word play with the lawyers," he said.

"After all, it can get a bit dreary in some cases and you need a bit of light relief here and there to stop the jury falling asleep."

★ A YOUNG punk in St Kilda proved this week that reality is funnier than fiction when he tried to hitch a ride on a private tram used as a mobile venue for the *Storming St Kilda By Tram* performances.

The unscheduled performance occurred when the tram stopped in Domain Rd, Sth Yarra, to let one of the character actors on. The spikey-haired punk, mistaking the vehicle for a real tram, attempted to get on. The doors would not open for him so he hung on to the running board screaming "Let me in" until the next stop.

Gaining entry, he screamed abuse at the "conductor" — and the audience, thinking he was part of the show, laughed.

The punk alighted at the next stop, commenting that he'd never seen such a rude bunch. The audience, of course, applauded him.

# BEST WEEKEND

## THEATRE

Melbourne's dynamic theatre scene provides drama for all tastes.

There are traditional big-budget productions at the **Princess**, the **Comedy** and **Her Majesty's** (shows like the long-running *CATS* and the current conservative comedy *Wife Begins at Forty*). The **Melbourne Theatre Company's** repertory work at the **State Theatre** (*Les Liaisons Dangereuses* with Angela Punch McGregor and John Stanton is playing there this month) is expected to liven up somewhat this season with more showing the contemporary Australian theatre scene to audiences overseas. On May 4, it will mount a revival of its successful 1983 production of Lawler's *Summer of the Seventeenth Doll* at the Athenaeum.

The next production offered by **The Australian Contemporary Theatre**, which works out of the Church Theatre in Hawthorn, is a Jacobean comedy, *Volpone* by Ben Johnson. It starts on April 29 and includes Rhys McConnochie, who is active in NSW television and theatre, Genevieve Picot, who is president of Actors Equity, and Ernie Grey, well-known in their previous production, *Storming Mont Albert by Tram*, Theatreworks is currently *Storming St Kilda by Tram* in a piece of theatre originally planned for The Age Comedy Festival and now running till at least the end of this month. The company mounts theatre of everyday life, encouraging audiences to think differently about the quality of their existence. *Get the Lady a Drink*, by VCA writing school graduate Jenni Hill, being staged in August, is about women and drinking; *On Shifting Sandshoes*, in November, is about beach holidays with a dose of politics thrown in.

Peter Oyston, are battling to the old CUB malthouse in Street rebuilt as a theatre to re the original devastated by fire years ago, and still find the en to mount a solid season interesting theatre every Then there is **La Mama**, w has been providing space innovative and experim theatre for two decades; **Whistling in the Theatre**, o several small and innovative gr of actors which play diffe venues.

**Theatre Allsorts** ("all sort theatre for all sorts of peop allows theatregoers to subscrib a flexible group of product mounted by Anthill, the Chu La Mama, Playbox Theatreworks. You buy a boo of five vouchers which you redeem over the following months for a ticket to one play each company. Contact Playbox box office, Shop 46, Collins Street, City, or 650 4859.

Something completely diffe is Mairéid Sullivan's L **Performance Tours** (870 71) Designed for groups, the dayli tours take in a variety of shows restaurants worked out accord to your taste and budget. Y might start with a ride on a thea tram, then go on to lunch with l entertainment, spend the afterno at theatre workshops or a matin and have a pre-theatre dinn with live classical music as accompaniment, then go bucksta to meet the people behind scenes of a play, then on to supper show. "You're not we out at the end of it. You're well-f and it's all paced with plenty time," Sullivan says. A sin herself, she aims to provide "mo quality work for performe

Theatreworks uses unusual venues — the company's current production storms St Kilda by tram.

experimental and irreverent performances under the eye of new director Roger Hodgman. Amateurs are mounting a variety of shows around the suburbs, and here are many small innovative companies who live lean and aim rustically high.

A primary objective of **The Australian Nouveau Theatre**, the home of which is the Anthill Theatre in South Melbourne, for example, is to "stimulate and encourage audiences through presenting innovative theatre of excellence". Flamboyant French director Jean-Pierre Mignon has een challenging audiences since 1980, when he formed the ompany with Bruce Kellor, with hom he had worked at the old am Factory and La Mama. Last ar, the company had a core group ' five actors. This year, the rangement has been pared down cause of funding constraints and fers a program which includes Shakespearean roles. The five-year-old company produces or co-produces six plays a year and aims to explore serious theatre "through a popular base", to create a high level of actor-audience contact and a sense of each production being an "event", and to provide an opportunity for rising young artists and theatre technicians to work with seasoned professionals. Artistic director John Ellis co-founded the group with Lois Ellis, and now works alongside production director Robert Gerbert and administrator Julia Sutton. You can support the company by becoming a financial member or by joining its "Friends" group.

**Theatreworks** is based in Acland Street, St Kilda. Its directors, Paul Davies and Caroline Howard, have staged works in unusual venues, including a hotel, a living room and, very successfully, a tram. Following

Friends of Theatreworks, $10 a year, provides members with a newsletter and concessions.

Another important name, of course, is the **Playbox**. Its directors, Carillo Gantner and

Australian Contemporary Theatre staff, from left, Sally Beck, Robert Gebert, Julia Sutton, John Ellis and Kelly Parry.

someone in a show at night, fo example, might perform for one my tours during the day to ear some extra money". Groups of 2 say, can expect to pay about $12 each for a day's trip.

# Peg Morgan's Spotlight

## Tram storms St Kilda again

TRAMS. They provide useful transport to and from a show. But a tram as the theatre?

"Why not" thought that highly imaginative company Theatre Works back in 1983, and proceeded to stage a hit production *Storming Mont Albert by Tram*.

When they moved to the southern suburbs, it was a matter of writing a new script, changing the route and they had *Storming St Kilda by Tram*.

This proved one of the great successes of the 1988 Comedy Festival, selling out before opening night and awarded the Best Community Theatre Piece.

Now, it's back with the script revised by author Paul Davies to make it funnier than ever.

Mark Shirrefs, directing his third "Tram Show", has assembled one of the most talented comedy casts.

The travellers meet Siobhan Tuke the hapless conductress; Carole Patullo as Samantha Heart-Byrne the socialite; Louis Dingemans (Terry the Punk) and John Concannon as Nigel Davidson the Sydney film-maker.

The company promises patrons "the ride of their lives".

The Tram leaves the St Kilda Beach Terminus (opposite Luna Park) at 8.27 pm Mondays to Saturdays, with a 4.27 pm matinee also on Saturdays. Inquiries to Theatre Works, 534 4879; bookings on 650 1500 and BASS.

● "Goodness, is that beard for real?" say Tim and Andy Macdougall at the Storming St Kilda By Tram party. Roger Selleck, right, assures them it is.

## THE TRAM SHOW

## · THEATRE ·

# Trams, snakes and tea-cake

### · PAULA CARR ·

**STORMING ST KILDA BY TRAM**
**Luna Park Tram Stop, Tram No 902**

ONE does not expect to find the words 'entertainment' and 'tram' in the same sentence. On those long, seemingly endless journeys through Melbourne the traveller either drifts into introspection or otherwise casts voyeuristic glances over their fellow commuters and listens to their conversations. Where is that old lady going? Are the young man and the pretty girl in the next seat lovers? Friends? Siblings? Why are they fighting? Why is that man carrying a TV aerial and a woman's sun hat? Will that pregnant woman have twins?

TheatreWorks' current production Storming St Kilda by Tram written by Paul Davies and directed by Mark Shirrefs, panders to the voyeur in us all, and does so with great humour and panache. The entertainment takes place aboard a tram journeying from St Kilda to Young and Jacksons' Hotel then back to St Kilda. At the Ackland Street terminus the audience is invited aboard by a sassy tram 'connie' Alice Katrunski (played by the effervescent Sioban Tuke) and you just know that it is going to be an eventful trip. Safety p...

The last two characters in the production are Morris Stanley (Roger Selleck), the raincoated tram inspector ... ...enchant for illuminated bow ties ... ... For Constable ...yed by around Melbourne ... these events require participation than theatre. The struct... developed around ... which unfold in fro... audience, (who ne... into the fracas, due ... audience to the ac... ure in actuality sh... the lives of the cha... to participate in t... The character and off the tram at various stops, and the resultant interplay between them, via a circuitous route, into the city. Unlikely characters get on... types, and Davie ween them creates a lively and not too far removed from reality prejudices, prec... entertainment. The interval is observed at Young and Jacksons, and... traffic in order to dem... your ticket entitles you to a free beer.

As the various producers of the recent spate of 'garden' plays are ...nces in well aware, there is nothing like an unusual venue or setting to ...acteriza-tillate the palate of the jaded theatre-goer; Loving Friends extend... tion was ed their season until February 14th, Wind In The Willows has been... dramatic going for five years, and even Theatresports are launching their new... the tram season in the Botanical Gardens. Storming St Kilda By Tram,... sound. Melbourne's only perambulatory theatrical entertainment, has also... returned for the third time, with a new cast and re-written script, ... ... ems when As with most truly successful ideas, the premise is mouthwater... away from ingly simple. The audience join the tram in St Kilda, which takes inevitable ... ... d space of ... ... ... ... or attention ...

The plot strands are simple but engaging: Storming St Kilda is a ...le moments humour of the mobile soap opera. The acting is all excellent, especially Louis reactions of the cliched im Dingemans (former Cabbage Brother), as the appealing punk who ...cent cars, as world. There is falls in love with the Conductor (Sioban Tuke). From the moment ...ted from the by the laconic he explodes onto the tram clutching a stolen plastic dog, he antics on the and an invete dominates the show. Also notable are Taya Straton as she stoically his experi... fends off the attentions of her yuppy ex-boyfriend who has reap... ought to mind credibility. H... peared after a nine-year absence, and Carole Patullo as the snotty out Memories, permanent n... society woman who couldn't find a taxi. ...ary train filled disgust of ... Storming St Kilda is a marvellous show with obviously limited ...nicative, mun-... seating that it is worth booking ahead for. Much pleasure comes from ...ing across the - way to t... when the drama spills over to the outside of the tram — when one... I second train in (ullo) at... who has alighted — because the expressions on the faces of people... pull swing. The :k dr... on the street is absolutely priceless. Indubitably the most fun you ... ng champagne, ...blems, and ...can have on the Met.

★ Fiona Scott-Norman

...ite glass, is a snooty rich twi... ...ses O'Rourke of being a parasite. The ... is apparent. ...el Davidson, well groomed yuppie ...are all these rich folk doing ...ng trams?) and archetypal con ... is unexpectedly confronted with his friend, Cathy Waterman, who has ...entally suffered the same ... ...has not experienced ...l success as Nig... ons whiz ... d in ...

"After all, it can get a bit dreary in some cases and you need a bit of light relief here and there to stop the jury falling asleep."

A YOUNG punk in St Kilda proved this week that reality is funnier than fiction when he tried to hitch a ride on a private tram used as a mobile venue for the Storming St Kilda By Tram performances.

The unscheduled performance occurred when the tram stopped in Domain Rd, Sth Yarra, to let one of ...ned ... ferry is a ... ...udience's fantasies of being mugged-raped-murdered on public transport but his story, not surprisingly, has an unexpected twist when he falls for Alice the 'connie'.

# Tram to storm St Kilda again

TRAMS. They provide useful transport to and from a show. But a tram as the theatre?

"Why not?" thought that highly-imaginative company TheatreWorks, back in 1983, and proceeded to stage a hit production, Storming Mont Albert by Tram on one of the good old green rollers.

When they moved to the southern suburbs, it was a matter of writing a new script, changing the route and they had Storming St Kilda by Tram.

This proved one of the great successes of the 1988 Comedy Festival, selling out before opening night and gaining the Best Community Theatre Piece award.

Now, it's back with the script revised by author Paul Davies to make it even funnier. "Tram Show", Mark Shirrefs, directing his third comedy casts, has assembled one of the most talented comedy casts. The travellers meet Siobhan Tuke as Samantha Heart-conductress; Carole Patullo as Louis Dingemans (Terry the Byrne the socialite; Louis Dingemans (Terry the Punk) and John Concannon as Nigel Davidson the Sydney film-maker.

There's a ticket inspector of course, played by Roger Selleck, and a policewoman, portrayed by Sally-Anne Upton.

Others in the cast are Taya Straton and Cliff Ellim.

Describing it as "a moving piece of theatre", the company promises patrons "the ride of their lives".

...is a miser... ...the character actors on. The spikey-haired punk, mistaking the vehicle for a real tram, attempted to get on. The doors would not open for him so he hung on to the outside board screaming "Let me in" until the next stop.

Gaining entry he screamed abuse at the 'conductor' — and the audience, laughed that he'd never seen the show. The punk alighted at the next stop, commenting that the tram was part of the Storming St Kilda By Tram performance. The such a rude bunch. The audience, of course, applauded him.

...with a Lady ... of ...

THE TRAM SHO[W]

**STORMING ST KILDA BY TRAM was awarded the AWGIE for "best Community Theatre Piece"**

"This show has everythin[g]"
The Melbourne Times

"Making mirth on the move"
Helen Thomson- The Australian

Tram ride with a difference.

TRAM-LOAD OF LAUGHS

"STORMING ST KILDA BY TRAM works because it is essentially true. It's all very funny and a fine time is had by all. Don't miss this show." - The Herald

"Mark Shirrefs keeps the action moving at a pace and schedule that Metrail can only dream of!" - The Age.

"You're bound to enjoy this robust slice of Melbourne life".
The Australian.

"One of the most surreal events to animate Melbourne Theatre." Jack Hibbard, The Age.

TRAM RIDE PROVES MOVING THEATRE
-SOUTHERN CROSS

# THE TRAM SHOW

## Arts and Entertainment

# Soap opera on wheels

**All aboard the tram**

STORMING ST KILDA BY TRAM
By Paul Davies
Theatreworks
Review: CHRIS BOYD

**THEATRE**

As TheatreWorks enters its second decade, it is about to embark upon the third phase of its history.

When founded, in 1980, the company went about providing Melbourne's Eastern suburbs with community theatre. Five years later, TheatreWorks relocated to Acland Street in St Kilda where it has become a near indispensable part of the local bohemian spirit.

This latest return season of *Storming St Kilda By Tram*, one of the company's earliest and most enduring works, marks the end of TheatreWorks as we know it. The first time the show was mounted, the destination was Mont Albert. The cast for that first production reads like a who's who of TheatreWorks. Paul Davies, Caz Howard, Peter Sommerfield, Peter Finlay and Hannie Rayson.

Following Paul Davies' resignation, late last year, Robert Draffin has been appointed as TheatreWorks' artistic director.

Draffin, one of this country's most gifted directors, will quite literally transform the company. It is an exciting and unexpected move by the TheatreWorks board. More information on the company's new direction should be available in coming weeks.

The latest incarnation of *Storming St Kilda* has a new cast (Cliff Ellen excepted), several new gags, and a different ending. Paul Davies has polished his script. His talent for one-liners gets better each year! "Time wounds all heels," an escort agency worker's says to her jerk ex-boyfriend.

*Storming St Kilda by Tram* works because it is essentially true. We've all watched eccentric travellers and listened to arguments which grew too loud to remain private. This show simply multiplies the familiar and enhances the banal, through the introduction of funny lines.

*All aboard while smoking a cigarette, is the call during the play Storming St Kilda by Tram, at the St Kilda Terminus, which starts on Friday February 1.*

MELBOURNE'S tramway system is one of the nine wonders of the world, according to local and overseas commuters who regard it as something special.

Something special also applies to the play *Storming St Kilda by Tram*, which starts its season on Friday February 1. The play will be staged on a tram which departs the St Kilda terminus, cnr Ackland and Upper Esplanade, St Kilda Monday to Saturday at 8.27pm. It is being produced under the guidance of the Theatreworks Group.

Spokeswoman Georgie Howitt said the play captured the imagination of everyone who had ever ridden on the Met with its realism, wit and original lines.

She said theatregoers would be able to see the production while travelling along some of the most scenic routes on the National Heart Foundation tram.

The cast includes outer fringe members, Siobhan Tuke, Cliff Ellen, Sally-Anne Upton, Carole Patullo, Louis Dingemans and Taya Straton.

*Storming St Kilda by Tram and tramming up a storm: the TheatreWorks cast whoops it up on wheels.*

Davies' observations on contemporary society, too, are getting more pungent and wryly perceptive. The ex-boyfriend, for example, a chic "filmmaker" from Sydney, talks of a course in group therapy he took by correspondence. (Think about it!).

In previous years, I have complained that the scripts of these locational theatre events have, in general, been underwritten and thus productions have relied too heavily on the environment. With this latest version of *Storming St Kilda*, with tram and the script are perfectly matched. The play couldn't exist without the location - and vice versa.

*Storming St Kilda by Tram* is a soap-opera-buffa-cabaret on wheels. It will delight once-a-week theatregoers no less than once-a-year punters. Do yourself a favour...

# Author

Paul Davies is an award winning screenwriter, script editor and playwright who sharpened his quill on over a hundred episodes of Teledrama from classic Crawford series such as *Homicide* (1974-5), *The Box* (1975-76) *The Sullivan's* (1976-78) and *Skyways* (1979), to *Rafferty's Rules* (1985), *Blue Heelers* (1997), *Pacific Drive* (1996), *Stingers* (1998-2003), *Something in the Air* (1999-2001) and *Headland* (2005). He also helped spark the site-specific performance revolution in Melbourne in the 1980s with TheatreWorks' production of his first play *Storming Mont Albert By Tram* (1982). What became known as *The Tram Show* played across a dozen years to packed trams in both Melbourne and Adelaide, travelling a total distance that would have taken the show halfway round the world. Its success lead to an outbreak of 'location theatre' in Melbourne throughout the 1980s including three other plays in real places: *Breaking Up In Balwyn* (1983, on a riverboat), *Living Rooms* (1986, in an historic mansion) and *Full House/No Vacancies* (1989, in a boarding house). These works became the subject of his thesis *Really Moving Drama*.

Both *The Tram Show* and *On Shifting Sandshoes* (1988) were awarded AWGIES, along with *Return of The Prodigal* (2000) an episode of *Something In The Air* (ABC). Paul co-wrote the feature *Neil Lynn* with David Baker in 1984, and the docufiction *Exits* (1980) with Pat Laughren and Carolyn Howard. His novel, *33 Postcards From Heaven* was published by Gondwana Press in 2005. Numerous articles, reviews, stories and interviews have been published in *Metro, Cinema Papers, Cantrill's Filmnotes, Australasian Drama Studies, Community Theatre In Australia, The Macquarie Companion to the Australian Media* and *Theatre Research International* (Cambridge University). He co-wrote three documentaries with John Hughes (*All That Is Solid, Traps and One Way Street*) as well as *Holy Rollers* with Rosie Jones. Paul has also given courses in literature and creative writing at various colleges and universities including: Southern Cross, James Cook and Melbourne State.

Photo Ruth Maddison

www.ingramcontent.com/pod-product-compliance
Lightning Source LLC
Chambersburg PA
CBHW071916290426
44110CB00013B/1382